'ALL STATIONS TO
LONGRIDGE'

'ALL STATIONS TO LONGRIDGE'

A History of the Preston to Longridge Branch Line and Associated Railways

David John Hindle

AMBERLEY

This book is dedicated to our first grandchild
James David Edward Lazell, born 6 October 2010

Cover illustrations: front cover (top) Stanier 2-8-0 No. 48679 passes the
remains of Deepdale Station (Alan Castle); front cover (bottom) Stanier
Class 5 4-6-0 No. 44874 alongside Courtalds' No. 2 ground frame; back
cover Stanier 4-6-0 No. 45212 shunting alongside the site of the demolished
Maudland Curve Signal Box (Alan Castle)

Frontispiece: Ordnance Survey Map of 1924 showing the Preston-Longridge
branch line. Principal stations were situated at Deepdale, Ribbleton,
Grimsargh and Longridge. At Grimsargh the line to Whittingham Hospital
veered off to the north east. The meandering River Ribble closely paralleled
the railway to the south.

First published 2010

Amberley Publishing
Cirencester Road, Chalford,
Stroud, Gloucestershire, GL6 8PE

www.amberleybooks.com

British Library Cataloguing in Publication Data.
A catalogue record for this book is available from the British Library.

ISBN 978 1 4456 0200 4

Typesetting and Origination by Amberley Publishing.
Printed in Great Britain.

Contents

A typical enough scene during the final decades of the Preston & Longridge Railway's existence, Stanier 8F 2-8-0 No 48438 ex-Courtaulds' Red Scar Works, is seen passing the ornate Cromwell Road Bridge in Ribbleton on 4 July 1966. Courtesy: Peter Fitton

The oil painting by local artist Joseph O'Donnel shows Barclay side tank 0-4-2 outside Whittingham Station. The Whittingham Hospital railway was linked to the Longridge line at Grimsargh. (David Hindle Collection)

Acknowledgements

Research has encompassed a wide range of primary sources. I acknowledge the help of staff at the National Archive, Kew, London; National Railway Museum, York; Harris Reference Library, Preston; Lancashire Record Office (LRO) and the Signalling Record Society, who have all offered advice and furnished valued sources of archived material. Journalists of yesteryear wrote about the social impact of railways on local communities, as well as detailing aspects of railway workings. These primary sources provide a light-hearted, retrospective look at the Victorian steam railway, and the *Preston Chronicle* (1812), *Preston Pilot* (1825), *Preston Guardian* (1844) and the *Lancashire Daily Post* have all been scrutinised.

I especially acknowledge the help and expertise of Mike Atherton, Brian Bamber, Alan Castle, Robert Gregson, Tom Heginbotham, John Holmes, R. H. Hughes (Manchester Locomotive Society), Derek Hicks, Andrew Mather, Mike Norris, Garth Sutcliffe, Martin Willacy, George Whiteman, Alan Wilding and accredited photographers including Peter Fitton, Alan Castle, David Eaves, Martin Hilbert, Tony Gillett, Alan Middleton, Gordon Biddle, Linda and Hugh Barton, Ian Race, Ian Grayston, Alan Summerfield and Richard Casserley (son of the renowned railway photographer, the late H. C. Casserley, for permission to use his father's photographs); also to Rebecca Woollam for her patience with the preparation of photographic material. Taped interviews from those familiar with the railway have yielded technical and anecdotal material and numerous contributors have provided valued material photographs and documents, including Mrs Frances Wright, the widow of Mr Gilbert Wright, the last driver on the Whittingham line and members of Longridge & District Local History Society. I thank all contributors, while pointing out that I have made every effort to trace copyright owners of material and apologise if any acknowledgements have been omitted. Finally, I would like to thank my publisher for making this work possible.

Foreword

Of the several books that he has previously produced, the writings of David Hindle encompass incredibly diverse ranges of topic, with ornithology, local history, fell walking, and even Preston's music halls being among an impressive repertoire. However, as a railway enthusiast, being raised – and still residing – within sight and sound of the much lamented tracks that once connected the small Lancashire town of Longridge with the outside world at Preston, the history of that locality and its railway undoubtedly has always been David's personal forte.

Certainly, all that you are about to read is the culmination of many years' research, resulting in the production of what is certainly the definitive account of a diminutive and sleepy branch line that once aspired to far greater ambitions, along with a unique approach to the subject that many will appreciate as providing a quite engrossing essay in social history.

David's path first crossed with my own during that very special year of 2008, at a time when the 40th anniversary of the very end of British Railways' steam was being commemorated. A series of events to mark such a landmark date had quite remarkably brought together a large number of both enthusiasts and former railwaymen alike, perhaps merely for no real reason other than an excuse to rekindle old friendships and to share with each other fond reminiscences of happier times!

Although there was a general acceptance by all that the glorious era of 'real' steam was irrevocably gone, those gatherings did demonstrate in the clearest manner possible that such days would never be entirely forgotten and that there would ever be a burning desire for nostalgia. Certainly, it is an undeniable fact that, with even long-vanished and now almost-forgotten rustic backwaters invariably proving to possess absorbing and colourful histories, there are still many stories out there just waiting to be told ... the Preston & Longridge Railway certainly proving to be no different in that respect!

It is a fact that my own initial encounter with the line was rather dramatic. Its existence did, in fact, manifest itself upon a pal and I one summer's day in the mid-1950s when, as schoolboy loco-spotters, we were engaged in earnestly seeking out a vantage point somewhere in the vicinity of Maudlands Goods Yard; hopeful of observing across the main line the movements on and off our celebrated personal 'Mecca' which was Preston's Croft Street Motive Power Depot. Scurrying through arguably dubious backstreets – mostly then still paved with stone setts and along which stretched mile upon mile of 'two-up, two-down' terraced dwellings, a pall of smoke spiralling into the air seemed to indicate to us the general direction of our ultimate goal and held definite promise of rewards about to unfold.

Suddenly the air was rant with the clamour of squealing flanges, clanging buffers and the beat of a freight train rapidly accelerating away from some unseen junction … and, evidently, in our general direction. We espied the walls of a railway under-bridge and, hopeful of an early acquisition of the first of many 'cops' of the day, dashed towards this. To actually obtain the loco number, an inevitable 'bunk-up' onto the parapet soon resulted in us both being seated in anticipation, with legs astride smoke-blackened coping stones. Way down below us lay a deep-walled cutting, spanned by similar thoroughfares a few yards away in either direction and from underneath, the nearest one of which a veritable volcano of skyward pyrotechnics was already erupting. Within seconds, a shower of still red-hot cinders descended from the heavens, followed by a blanket of thick, clinging grey fug that blotted out the whole area, leaving us both diving for cover and literally gasping for air.

To our ultimate disgust, and obvious exasperation, that loco hadn't even possessed a front number-plate! For some obscure reason, the ex-LNWR 0-8-0s (or 'Coffee Pots' – as we kids used to describe the ten or so of the former G2 class based at 10B Preston shed) never had done and, as was inevitably the case, the cab-side numerals on this one were also totally undecipherable; therefore the sole object of the exercise ultimately proved to have been well and truly thwarted! That aside, the vision of this vociferous 'Super D', accompanied by its such forthright demonstration of raw, unbridled power, had definitely created a lasting impact and one that, later, would always spring to mind whenever the Longridge branch came to be mentioned.

A gem of information, curiously imparted to us in the first instance by no other than my pal's dad (whose interest in transport matters normally did not extend beyond his undeniably encyclopaedic knowledge of anything and everything 'motor bike'), was the quite amazing revelation that a genuine ex-Southern Railway tank locomotive had been permanently exiled to work on an isolated branch line located somewhere near the village of Whittingham!

Incredulous though this news might at first have seemed, once we had established that the engine's number did not in actual fact appear in the current Ian Allan 'ABC' (nor had it done so for many a year), I am forced to admit that interest did wane somewhat. Nevertheless, what really came to be to my eternal regret is the fact that a relatively short bike ride might very well have secured the opportunity to discover one of the most unusual, if not absolutely unique, examples of passenger motive power anywhere in the country ... accompanied by the chance to travel totally free-of-charge in the sort of archaic 4-wheeled rolling stock that had already all but disappeared even in our grandparents' day!

As David's text will reveal, utilising for the final days of its existence a Sentinel 4-wheel geared vertical-boilered tank loco, the Whittingham Hospital Railway was certainly an anachronism ... indeed, this was a description that might have been considered equally pertinent at any previous point in the line's sixty-eight years of operation! The saddest fact of all is that, ultimately, all I got to see of the former line was a fleeting glimpse from the footplate of a passing locomotive of the one-time WHR waiting shelter and platform at Grimsargh, latterly in use as part of a builder's yard and long after all other traces had been well and truly obliterated.

However, back to the 0-8-0s – through the trackside grapevine I came to learn of a forthcoming enthusiasts' rail tour planned to start out from Preston and, not only was a 'Super D' booked to work one of the initial stages of this but, for lucky passengers-to-be, there were numerous other delights in store. The adventurous itinerary promised a unique chance to venture along many local byways that, even that far back in time, had not seen passenger trains in many a year ... indeed, in the case of Longridge, not since 1954 – when even that had been a similar one-off special excursion.

It was Springs Branch depot's still-surviving No. 49451 that came to be sent up to Lostock Hall shed a few days prior to the event 'for cleaning' – a task in which a few of us volunteered to assist. Although the trip had been optimistically entitled the 'Mid Lancs Railtour', such a designation was evidently somewhat of a misnomer, for both the itinerary notes and my Ian Allan *Pre-Grouping Atlas & Gazetteer* clearly confirmed that, apart from some ingeniously organised gyrations around the afore-ascribed county, we were also to delve deep into the Yorkshire Dales, indeed reaching as far as a Midland Railway outpost going by the name of Grassington & Threshfield, of which I then knew nothing. And, how we got to that branch terminus after arriving at Longridge with our little train of five ex-LMS coaches is quite a story in itself, but needless to say, such a journey might well have been possible by quite a different route, had the aspirations of one small railway company actually been realised ... but, of that aspect, I shall again leave it up to David to elaborate upon.

Eventually, I was particularly fortunate in being able to negotiate for a couple of quite unofficial footplate rides on the surviving steam-hauled freight trip-working that still ventured to the end of the line. All of three and a half decades after passenger trains had disappeared, a once-daily goods train incredibly still managed to serve one or two wayside sidings, delivering the occasional wagon-load of coal and dropping off the odd parcel or item of farm machinery here and there. In such a respect, Longridge Station proved to be a veritable time-warp – still permanently staffed, fully signalled and totally complete in every respect,

Following the fire at Preston engine-shed on 28 June 1960, it was goodbye to one old trouper that was no stranger to the Longridge line. With its connecting rods removed ex-LNWR Class 7F 0-8-0 No. 49196 stands forlornly in Maudland yard. Courtesy: Robert Gregson

From the footbridge serving St Maria Goretti's School, an enthusiastic group of homeward-bound schoolchildren watch WD 'Austerity' Class 2-8-0 No. 90675 as it approaches Gamull Lane Bridge at Ribbleton on 22 August 1964. Courtesy: Alan Castle

other than, perhaps, for its name-boards ... and a few intending passengers to stand waiting on its platforms! Travelling with the crews, firing a few rounds of coal, taking the odd photograph and even assisting in opening and closing of the several crossing gates *en route*, what better way could there ever have been to pass a leisurely day out in the country?

The search for the more unusual in pictorial opportunities soon led me to explore potential locations along the trackside and I retain in particular the memories of one memorable winter's day in 1966 when I chased 'No. 78 Target', being successful in obtaining pictures of the 8F and its lengthy train in four different places – all of which were amazingly achieved by a means of transport consisting of nothing more than a push-bike! Ah, happy days indeed!!

In the twenty-first century and passing into an age when both steam locomotives and branch lines have come to be considered as a creation of a more primitive era and quite simply are felt to deserve no place in such an adventurous period of new technology as now exists, for those who can take the time to cogitate upon such matters, there is a sadness felt today that reflects an acknowledgement that life as many of us once knew it has changed radically, perhaps for the better, perhaps not, but certainly with a realisation that those changes have been inevitable and do count as 'progress'. Set against such a background, the steam engine and the rural outposts that it once so faithfully served had inevitably been faced with only one ultimate destiny.

For those that knew the railway to Longridge intimately, it has gone forever, but it will never be forgotten!!

Alan Castle
January 2010

Introduction

I have always been fascinated by railways – not particularly in a train spotting kind of way, but for the sheer magic of the steam era, the journey itself and most especially the history of local branch lines and their impact on the rural communities they served. In writing this chronological history of the Preston & Longridge Railway (PLR), I have been drawn to both primary and secondary sources as detailed in the bibliography. The fruits of my labour take account of early transport systems and the first railways to open around Preston; thus connecting with the origins of the PLR and its social, economic and cultural use up to the date of complete closure of the remnant truncated line in 1994. These factors, together with the incorporation of new anecdotal material and photographs, will help to differentiate this book from similar studies.

The first railways were crucial in transforming the social and economic prosperity of the country's towns and villages, and the Preston & Longridge Railway was no exception. Close to my home, at the rear of the long-disused Ribbleton Station, before being replaced by a new generation of diesels, steam locomotives regularly thundered by, hauling the daily goods trains to Longridge. For me the branch was the epitome of a rural branch line and, despite its modest credentials, it has a particularly fascinating and complex history.

The PLR was, at first, an independent concern under the title of The Preston & Longridge Railway Company. It was first conceived in 1835 with the intention of linking quarries situated at the western end of Longridge Fell with a distribution centre at Deepdale Street, close to Preston town centre. Preston's place as a forerunner of national railway growth coincided with the opening of this combined mineral and passenger line and it was on 1 May 1840 that the expanding town came to be linked with the village of Longridge, six and a half miles to the north-east. Following the arrival of the North Union Railway in 1838, the branch was, chronologically, only the second railway to open in the Preston area and, in fact, preceded even the Lancaster & Preston Junction Railway that was to evolve into the main Anglo-Scottish route.

A contemporary account of the opening in the *Preston Chronicle* of 2 May 1840, however, alludes to delays in construction and that, at Longridge, a tunnel had to be constructed in order that the line could enter the most productive quarries. Eight years before the age of steam, genuine equine 'horse-power' was the means of propulsion up the steeply-graded route. The quarries at Longridge were situated about four hundred feet above sea level and the railway company exploited the natural contours of the land by using gravity for part of the return journey. The beasts of burden even gained a complimentary return ticket, before boarding their own special carriage to be conveyed back down the steep gradients to Grimsargh and beyond. The horses would then regain their place at the head of the train and haul the heavy loads on to Preston. In June 1848, it was 'all change' to steam traction and, thereafter, plumes of white smoke became a feature of the local landscape. The horses were pensioned off in the wake of this new technology and enjoyed a well-earned retirement in the tranquil fields of their home station at Grimsargh.

During a period of Victorian railway mania, the PLR almost graduated to main-line status, with an ambitious plan by a new consortium, the Fleetwood, Preston & West Riding Junction Railway Company, to link the line with the industries of West Yorkshire. The overall plan was aborted and only partial implementation was to reach fruition when the extension of the PLR from Maudland (Preston) to Deepdale Junction was completed in 1850. This was to be a catalyst for the Maudland link, which effectively saw trains entering Preston's main station in 1885. During 1852, the PLR claimed a significant first in the history of railway development. It had the distinction of being the first railway of all to fall within the tender care of bailiffs. However, in this case, the phoenix was to rise from the ashes.

Ongoing conjectures and counter-proposals for the future prosperity of the line leave me to wonder what rail travel was really like on the PLR in those halcyon days of the mid-nineteenth century and how much attention might have been paid to passenger comfort. The evidence confirms that, at the time of the opening, horses drew passengers in carriages about three times a week, but on other occasions passengers were conveyed on a seat screwed to the rear buffers of a stone wagon. With the advent of steam, a contemporary newspaper report in 1849 (see Chapter 6) described a 'primitive country railway worked by old asthmatic engines and a 1st class passenger sharing a passenger compartment with a 1st class bovine'. This could only happen on the Longridge line, I think!

Consequently it emerges that the railway, in serving an agricultural community, was looked upon in some quarters with a mixture of amusement and affection, prompting correspondents to write tongue-in-cheek letters to newspapers, reporting upon such bizarre occurrences. This surprising level of eccentricity was not without precedent, however, for, contiguous with the line at Grimsargh, was the equally unconventional and totally eccentric Whittingham Hospital Railway. The private WHR opened in June 1889. Henceforth, coal trains from Preston's industrial base at Deepdale Sidings destined for Whittingham were to be shunted directly into sidings situated behind Grimsargh Station. The Whittingham train carried passengers free of charge from those early beginnings. Thus, who could resist boarding the train at Grimsargh's quaint branch line station for a free ride to Whittingham? On arrival there were plenty of opportunities to explore the landscaped hospital gardens and watch a local sporting fixture. I personally discovered life on the inside when, in January 1960, I became a member of the hospital's workforce of over nine hundred and it was there that I met a young nurse, Dorothy Shorrock, whom I was destined to marry.

Above: Grimsargh Station in June 1948, with the LNWR Station behind the semaphore signal. Hospital workers board the train for Whittingham hauled by Barclay engine No. 2. Tom Heginbotham Collection

Right: David Hindle and Dorothy Shorrock at Whittingham, in October 1960 – the start of a blossoming romance.

On 12 April 1952, the Whittingham Hospital Railway's unique D1, 'James Fryars', was ready to depart from Grimsargh Station. Courtesy: A. Summerfield

The view from the footplate as an unidentified Stanier Class 8F 2-8-0 awaits the signals at Deepdale *en route* to Ribbleton with a coal train. Courtesy: Ian Race

Stanier Class 5MT 4-6-0 No. 45055 passes below Cromwell Road Bridge at Ribbleton and heads towards Courtaulds' Sidings on 31 July 1968. Courtesy: Chris Spring

Photographed at Deepdale, Stanier Class 8F 2-8-0 No. 48775 heads towards Ribbleton with a coal train destined for Courtaulds on 1 August 1968. Courtesy: Chris Spring

Out with the old, in with the new: On 16 April 1991, Class 37 No. 37.167 arrives at Deepdale Mill Street, Preston, with a train of coal hoppers *en route* to the coal distribution depot at Deepdale. Courtesy: Chris Spring

On the return journey, Class 37 No. 37.167 heads west, with an empty load from Deepdale Road, towards the Maudland tunnel on 16 April 1991. Courtesy: Chris Spring

Long before that, the extra freight and passenger traffic on the WHR boosted returns on the Longridge line, with both lines enjoying their social and economic heyday during the first two decades of the nineteenth century. Grimsargh once sustained two stations on separate lines. The hospital's private station was situated on the north side of Long Sight Lane, diagonally opposite the joint LNWR/LYR Station, which opened in 1870 on the south side of Long Sight Lane, adjacent to a level crossing. The trailing junction that linked the Longridge branch to the Whittingham line and station veered to the north of Grimsargh level crossing gates and, interestingly, was named 'Whittingham Junction' on the first Ordnance Survey maps.

The WHR passenger service eclipsed those on the PLR by twenty-seven years, and when the private line closed on 29 June 1957, the PLR was still supplying about 250 tons of coal to service the hospital's boilers. Consequently, during the last decade of the PLR, more valued freight traffic was lost. The phased withdrawal of freight services took place at Grimsargh and Longridge in 1967, Courtaulds' Factory in 1980 and, finally, Deepdale Sidings in 1994.

The Longridge and associated line to Whittingham symbolised rural railways of bygone Lancashire, with a forgotten scenario of quaint trains in a vanishing landscape. Retrospectively, there is a certain romanticism of those pre-Doctor Beeching days that now forms the basis of research into an untapped source of immensely interesting social history.

'The Prologue' – Preston and Stations to Longridge

The opening years of the twentieth century saw a king on the throne for the first time in sixty-four years, two world wars had yet to be fought and a liner named *Titanic* was to sink in the North Atlantic with tremendous loss of life. In Preston, electric tramcars were gradually replacing earlier forms of public transport and the motorcar had yet to revolutionise matters. Steam lorries were appearing on the scene and traction engines were replacing horses for the haulage of heavy industrial materials and for agricultural use.

Close by, at Preston Station, a new generation of powerful express steam locomotives, capable of hauling heavy loads, thundered by. Little notice would have been taken of a short train drawn up at the end of one of the departure platforms, for this would have little significance and status among those giants of the permanent way that now clanked into Preston resplendent with their new corridor coaches.

Nevertheless, the local service to Longridge was beginning to realise its potential as both a freight and passenger line. Generations of schoolchildren – and some adults – who watched the trains go by throughout the Victorian era, began to become aware that, just perhaps, there might be life beyond the villages of Longridge and Grimsargh after all. A prominent member of the Longridge community, Harry Clegg, whose forebears helped to reform the Longridge Brass Band as the St Lawrence's Brass Band in 1883, recalled a through excursion train in 1908: 'Whit Monday, 1908 was a wonderful day for us. It was a full train that left Longridge at 5-00am that sunny Whit Monday morning. Travel in those days was limited and going to North Wales was something of an expedition to local people. I remember the train coming to a halt at a Welsh wayside station, and the stationmaster announcing that the engine had broken down, and it would be at least an hour before a relief got through. Some of the male passengers were soon climbing the fence to visit the nearest pub. The stationmaster kindly promising that the engine driver would blow his whistle when it was time to go. Back in half the time, one of the men told the stationmaster: "No need to blow the whistle now, we've supped up". The lovely castle and fine buildings of Caernarvon delighted everyone, but the band needed more practice before going to the contest. Putting all they knew into a selection of sea shanties, the Longridge Band won first prize, their bandmaster, Mr Jack Clayton, receiving a silver cup, which was to become his own property in 1910'. [1]

Thus, in Edwardian times, through trains from Longridge were destined for exciting resorts such as Caernarvon, while fulfilling the social needs of the public. Reflecting further, let us now embark on a Longridge-bound train at Preston Station, for a guided tour of the branch. Within the context of the 'mists of time,' the precise date is unimportant, though like the above passage the period is early twentieth century.

Long ago, the wooden semaphore sign at Preston Station indicated 'All Stations to Longridge calling at Deepdale, Ribbleton, Grimsargh and Longridge'. All four stations had a residential element that provided important custom for the railway. Deepdale Bridge Station (1856) and Ribbleton Station (1854), situated on the outskirts of Preston, contrasted with the architectural style of Grimsargh (1870) and Longridge (1872) Stations, the latter being typical of the period of country branch LYR Stations.

Accordingly, we now board a short train headed by a Webb 2-4-2T – a typical steam locomotive that regularly worked the Longridge branch passenger service. After steaming out north along the main line for about half a mile, the train passes the site of Preston engine-shed and Preston No. 5 Signal Box, before entering the branch on a sharp right-hand curve. Passing the magnificent spire of St Walburge's Church, completed in 1867 and boasting the third highest steeple in the country, of interest is the fact that redundant limestone sleeper blocks from the original Lancaster & Preston Junction Railway were used in the construction of the lower part of the tower. After then passing under the first of several bridges, the train enters the western portal of the half-mile long Maudland ('Miley') Tunnel, where it is said that the occupants of the houses above regularly experienced the vibrations of steam engines passing far below.

Following the experience of exploring subterranean depths beneath the streets of Preston, the train emerges into a cutting alongside the 'Preston Royal

Infirmary'. This was formerly the 'House of Recovery', in respect of which the legislative process had decreed that the railway should not pass within 100 yards. Close by was one of Preston's earliest cinemas, the 'Victory', later known as the 'Rialto', which was constructed immediately adjacent to the PLR tracks. (There were even double seats there for courting couples, as I know only too well – but we digress!) Although it boasted 'the latest ventilating system, clean and free from smoke', the passage of steam trains nevertheless shook the place whenever any were so inconsiderate as to pass by.

Deepdale Bridge Station is now reached, with its entrance by means of a small street-level building. About one mile after leaving Maudland, the train then passes over Deepdale Junction and the double tracks converge into a single-line. At this point, a short section of double-track diverges backwards, to reach Deepdale Coal Sidings, where the original passenger and freight terminus of the Preston & Longridge Railway was situated. There were only two block-posts on the branch, Maudland Curve and Deepdale Junction. A block-post is usually a signal box, which controls the section ahead, to ensure that only one train is in that section at any one time. The 5 miles 922 yards section from Deepdale Junction to Longridge Level Crossing was worked as a single-line, using a round red staff; the staff station being located at Deepdale Junction.

Immediately after passing under the bridge carrying Blackpool Road, a short siding to the left once served a small brick-works and sand-pit owned by Thomas Croft and, latterly, in the 1960s, a Fyffe's banana warehouse. Just before Cromwell Road Bridge, Ribbleton, additional sidings were laid outside a large refrigerated building, constructed for the storage of emergency rations at the time of the Second World War.

In 1863, a short-lived Ribbleton Station was opened east of Cromwell Road Bridge and, in my childhood days, the original platform was still visible from a public footpath crossing that has since been closed, between Hamilton Road/ Stuart Road. Nearby, a plaque on the ornate Cromwell Road Bridge once stated that the Ribbleton Freehold Land Public Society built the bridge in 1863. However, modernisation of the structure in the 1980s obliterated the Victorian architecture and, for some inexplicable reason, the plaque was removed at the same time.

The highest embankment on the route bisected the valley of the Eaves Brook at Ribbleton and it was here that I watched the 'Super Ds' laboriously hauling their coal trucks towards Ribbleton Station, (originally called Gammer Lane Station) and where Gamull Lane Bridge spanned the single platform. A little further along the line, Messrs. Courtaulds' Red Scar works first became a blot on the rural landscape in 1938, when it opened as the largest man-made fibre plant in Europe, albeit simultaneously providing lifeblood to the PLR Courtaulds had its own one mile branch line, which led to the factory from Exchange Sidings alongside the Longridge branch.

Thereafter, our train passes over a short embankment and through a cutting alongside Grimsargh St Michael's Church, before passing under the bridge

At Gamull Lane, an unidentified Stanier loco is seen in the cutting passing St Maria Goretti's Church, Ribbleton. Courtesy: Alan Middleton

The same train heads north alongside St Maria Goretti's School, with heavily-laden coal trucks bound for Courtaulds' Sidings. Courtesy: Alan Middleton

'Watch that steam from Target 63' Stanier Class Five 4-6-0 No. 44761. The one-time countryside depicted here has now been transformed into the industrial urban expansion known as 'Preston East.' Courtesy: Alan Middleton

Stanier Class Five
4-6-0 No. 44761, runs
tender-first back to
Preston. Courtesy: Alan
Middleton

'Target 63', Stanier
Class 8F 2-8-0 No.
48775, at Courtaulds'
Exchange Siding, *c.*
1966. Courtesy: Alan
Middleton

Stanier Class 8F
2-8-0 No. 48476, in
unspoilt countryside
between Ribbleton
and Grimsargh,
c. 1966. Courtesy:
Alan Middleton

carrying Preston Road. Approaching Grimsargh Station the Level Crossing was
protected by signals, these being interlocked with the crossing gates. There were
also sidings on either side of the line at Grimsargh, firstly for the goods yard and
secondly for the asylum branch line, where points would be released by the train
crew using an 'Annett's key.'

Arriving at the old LMS Station at Grimsargh, the sight of stationmaster
Latham would have presented itself, emerging from his office to welcome
passengers. Anyone running for the train was usually accommodated, before
the driver opened the regulator of his engine. Beginning the gradual ascent to
Longridge the train now passes alongside Grimsargh Reservoir, the first of the
large reservoirs to be constructed for Preston during 1835, three years before the
opening of the PLR The single-track now segments a wilderness area of arable
land before reaching Shay Lane Crossing on the outskirts of Longridge. This
was the start of the steepest gradient on the line, which reached a maximum of
1 in 50 at the 40-yard long Stone Bridge tunnel at Longridge. Emerging from the
tunnel, a view of terraced houses with grey slate roofs unfolds, interspersed with
several mill chimneys and somehow integrated with a contrasting spectacular
backcloth of Longridge Fell and the rolling hills of the Forest of Bowland.

Our train finally enters Longridge Station, where just beyond double tracks
continued over Berry Lane level crossing, into the goods yard which had extensive
facilities for coal and the diverse needs of local industries. At this point, near an
occupation bridge, the 7-mile marker post on the shunting neck of the branch
was approached. A small section of the extended branch that led to the quarries
remained in use merely as a head-shunt for trains right up to the withdrawal of
freight facilities in 1967.

PART ONE

THE PLR IN THE VICTORIAN ERA

CHAPTER ONE

The Birth of a Transport Revolution

A concise social and economic background to Preston and Longridge during the Industrial Revolution is presented in this chapter, while a parallel line examines the growth of transport systems around Preston.

The River Ribble and the sharp contours of its valley have helped to preserve the relatively unspoilt countryside between Preston and Longridge, and industrialisation has, to this day, not impacted too heavily upon the landscape. There are still no bridges between the Preston boundary and Ribchester, for there was little incentive to build important roads alongside the north bank of the meandering river. Longridge nestles at the gateway to the Ribble Valley, where every house, farm earthwork, woodland and field boundary has its own story to tell, each reflecting human activity over many centuries.

The Roman road, Watling Street, linked forts at Ribchester near Longridge to Kirkham and the archaeological remains of the road ran close to the Longridge railway line, where the Romans and their livestock once hauled wooden trucks along the ancient highway. The Hundred of Amounderness, to the north of the Ribble, attracted many Norse settlers and many small villages owe their origins to the Norse colonies; the Viking influence being evidenced in the derivation of names of local villages. Grimsargh was originally the only intermediate station on the PLR and the name originates from a Norse settlement and agricultural hamlet. The name 'argh', or 'aerg', was probably an equivalent spelling for a summer farm, a cluster of wooden huts used for the shelter of cattle in summer. The name 'Grim' is derived from 'Grimr', which is a well-known Norseman's name. It is therefore likely that the land of the Norse township would have been in pasture and this was the argh or pasture of Grimr.

During the Middle Ages, warring factions and explorers negotiated the relatively gentle contours of the Wharfedale and Ribble Valley landscapes as an east-to-west route. The trans-Pennine crossing from the Vale of York to the Ribble estuary is traceable by a chain of Norman castles, including those at Skipton and Clitheroe. Both the Romans and Cromwell were quick to exploit the

The hollow alongside the dead tree indicates the course of the Roman Road at Elston, Grimsargh. The PLR crossed and paralleled the road at several points. David Hindle

'Greetings from Grimsargh'; an original postcard featuring aspects of Victorian Grimsargh and district. With the coming of the railway it seems almost as although Grimsargh had aspirations to become a tourist resort. Courtesy: Tom Heginbotham

The railway passed under the bridge carrying the Preston to Longridge road through Grimsargh. The building nearest to the bridge was the old St Michael's village school. Beyond is St Michael's Church, a prominent local landmark for railway passengers. Author's Collection

The Victorian railways brought about one of the most notable events in social history. The railway station at Grimsargh (photographed in the 1950s) was key for newly found adventure and travel. Author's Collection

strategic value and, indeed, Preston and Longridge do have strong associations with Cromwell. The route of the PLR is steeped in ancient and modern history, exemplified at Ribbleton where the highways include the names of officers who fought on Ribbleton Moor during the Battle of Preston of 17 August 1648. This was probably the most crucial conflict of the Civil Wars, which occurred throughout the British Isles from 1642 to 1651. Although it is not one of the best-known battles fought on English soil, few military actions have changed English history as dramatically as Oliver Cromwell's defeat of the Scottish army and the English Northern Royalists in Lancashire – for it was this conflict that brought the second Civil War to an abrupt end.

What Preston and Longridge did have in common was their close proximity to beautiful countryside, although at Preston it was often represented as a sliver of green fields and distant fells, perceived through a haze of smoke from factory, home and, of course, railway engines breathing smoke and sparks in the manner of fiery dragons. An early *Preston Chronicle* description of the route, to be enjoyed from the open carriage window on the PLR, alluded to the countryside of a bygone era and its historical associations with the Romans and the Battle of Preston in 1648: 'The line passes through interesting country and, as the train advanced, the elevated ground traversed afforded to those in the open carriages a beautiful view of the surrounding country. The day was beautifully fine and nature appeared in her most promising costume, meadow and cornfield, garden and orchard, giving hopes of a beautiful harvest. The route itself is not devoid of interest; nor is it barren of historical associations. The scene of Cromwell's battle with the parliamentary forces is but a short distance from the line, and it crosses the Roman road on which the soldiers of Rome journeyed on their way to the ancient city and port of Coccium, or Ribchester. Although looking comparatively modern, the church at Grimsargh (first built 1715) covered with ivy, is perhaps one of the most picturesque spots on the line. Hoghton tower, once the seat of baronial power and the scene of kingly revels crowns the wood grit hill to the right. Before us are the hills of Longridge and below us, Preston, with the chimneys and spires, and other evidence of industry and enterprise, and beyond it, the Ribble winding to the sea'.

Nowadays, Longridge is a thriving little town but, prior to the railway and the established quarrying and textile industries, was a straggling village consisting of a small number of irregularly-built terraced houses on Market Place, Higher Road and Berry Lane, the sixteenth century parish church of St Lawrence at Newtown. During the reign of William IV, the quarrying industry initially determined the strategic importance of the new PLR and its economy. Thomas Fleming, one of the principal quarry owners at Longridge, secured large-scale commercial quarrying operations and in 1821 a local historian penned a colourful account of this remarkable man and his enterprise: 'The Father of the Quarry Masters – a suit of clay coloured breeches, and a pair of clogs, was often enough the garb in which he was found by some of the wealthiest and most talented men of the

The valley at Ribbleton, where General Oliver Cromwell began battling with the Royalists in a crucial conflict of the Civil Wars, 'The Battle of Preston,' fought on 17 August 1648. Almost three hundred years later the landscape had been transformed into what was the most prominent embankment on the Longridge branch. The 'iron horse' of the twentieth century, Stanier 8F 2-8-0 No. 48679, is seen hauling its train towards Longridge. Courtesy: Alan Castle

Berry Lane is still the principal shopping street in Longridge and this 1930s view illustrates the location of the railway station (right) in relation to it. Courtesy: Longridge & District Local History Society

day. About this time, he made the acquaintance of the late Mr. Jesse Hartley, the talented and able Surveyor of the Liverpool Dock Company, with whom Mr. Fleming did considerable business. Colossal blocks were conveyed from Mr. Fleming's quarry to the docks at Liverpool. The enterprise and perseverance of Mr. Fleming, could, perhaps, never be placed in so favourable a light as at that period. There were no railways to connect the distant town of Liverpool with a remote village and the only mode of conveyance was by horse'. [2]

Around 1830, the expanding community of Longridge was progressively more closely associated with the growth of the commercial quarrying industry, which began to capitalise on the rich seams of ashlar stone. The export of enormous stone blocks involved incessant flows of horse-drawn wagons between Longridge and Preston and a more effective alternative to road transportation was sought. Thus, the quarry master Thomas Fleming was one of the promoters of the railway for the carriage of stone. Following the opening of the PLR in 1840, by the end of the nineteenth century the quarrying industry culminated in a total of twelve operational quarries.

The textile industry was mainly confined to the towns of industrial Lancashire and certain rural outposts including Longridge. With the coming of the railway, four cotton-weaving mills were built in the town between 1850 and 1874, the latter being situated alongside the line. Raw materials and cotton carried helped the textile industry to prosper and to carry on almost without stoppage, even during difficult times of economic restraint. As each mill opened, there was an expansion of terraced-housing in Longridge, especially along Berry Lane and streets adjacent thereto, which generated more passenger traffic for the railway, with many people arriving from both urban and rural areas. To meet the requirements of local industry, the railway was instrumental in transforming Longridge from a hamlet to a sprawling mill village by the end of the nineteenth century. The census returns show that, in 1841, there were approximately 1,006 people living in 191 houses, which had increased to 2,975 living in 659 houses by 1881. [3] Following the demise of the quarrying industry, a head-shunt extended from the level crossing on Berry Lane towards Victoria Mill. Victoria Mill was served by a short branch loop that ran straight through the mill with incorporated platforms undercover.

At the beginning of the Industrial Revolution, the social, economic and industrial foundation of Preston and outlying villages such as Longridge underwent considerable upheaval. Mills and factories dominated Preston throughout the Industrial Revolution and, consequently, during the period between 1831 and 1851 the population of Preston more than doubled to 69,542, increasing to 112,989 by 1901. During the first decades of the twentieth century, the reign of King Cotton prospered in Preston, but after the 1920s slump and the later competition from Asia, the textile industry never really recovered and, one by one, the cotton mills of Preston and Longridge came to face closure.

Transport Systems and Victorian Railway Development

It is key to consider the origin of the Preston to Longridge railway within the context of early forms of transport and Victorian railway development, thereby demonstrating its contribution as a pioneering mineral and passenger railway line during a period of Victorian railway mania. At the start of the Industrial Revolution, *c.* 1790, Preston was consuming around 20,000 tons of coal per annum and the importation of Wigan coal was essential. Construction work on a canal linking Kendal, Lancaster and Preston to the Wigan coalfields began in 1792 with John Rennie as the principal engineer. A simple plate-way and bridge across the Ribble was incorporated into the Director's plans to link the terminus of the Lancaster Canal at Marsh Lane, Preston to the Leeds Liverpool Canal at Walton Summit. Thus the very first railway in the Preston area was opened on 1 June 1803 as a mineral line linking the two canals.

At the time it was said: 'The first horse drawn train of six coal wagons was hosted by a band of music, and old and young left their habitations to witness a sight so novel'. Passenger traffic on the Lancaster Canal from Preston to Kendal ceased in 1846, after the opening of the Preston & Lancaster railway line in 1840, but continued for the conveyance of stone, coal and other goods. Although the Lancaster Canal was lock-free, because of the circuitous route taken by the canal in following the level contours, the boats were never as quick as the stagecoach.

The first stagecoach was introduced *c.* 1771 and ran between Preston and Warrington, via Wigan. This was followed by a coach running between Preston and Liverpool in 1774, for which the fare was expensive at 8s 6d. With the coming of the stagecoach, old roads had to be improved and turnpikes constructed. In 1824, a bridge was constructed over the River Ribble to carry the new turnpike from Preston to Blackburn. Towards the end of 1823, seventy-two stagecoaches left Preston every Wednesday, increasing to about 100 journeys a day by *c.* 1830. The direct stage service to London took two to three days, leaving Preston on a Monday at two o'clock. The last north-south mail coach through Preston ran during 1842.

A horse-drawn tramway was established in 1879, sanctioned by the Preston Tramways Company Limited. It ran for two and a half miles between Church Street and the Prince Albert Hotel, Fulwood, before being further extended by Preston Corporation in 1882 at a total cost of around £25,000. Attractions providing excellent custom for the railways included the immense popularity of the newly established Preston Pleasure Gardens in New Hall Lane. This late Victorian concept had widespread appeal and was accessible by rail and the established tramway network during Preston Guild 1882: 'Tram cars from all the railway platforms, direct to the (pleasure garden) gates, every few minutes'.[4] This might be perceived as an early form of integrated transport.

The tramway system was electrified after 1904, leading to the expansion and development of the outer suburbs. The stock comprised thirty-eight double-deck and ten single-deck cars that ran from Lancaster Road in the town centre, via North Road and Deepdale Road, to Sharoe Green Hospital and to Farringdon Park, Ashton, Broadgate and Ribbleton. W. Dick and J. Kerr established engineering works in 1897, in Strand Road, Preston, to meet the growing demands for tramcars and railway locomotives. Railways and tramcars were an important stimulus to the development of the outer suburbs when, by the end of the nineteenth century, new industries and better housing were established.

Preston's railways grew by successive amalgamations, from small local companies, to become part of much larger conglomerates and it is pertinent to see how the PLR evolved alongside the local railway network. The opening of Preston Station and the arrival of the line from Wigan on 31 October 1838 saw the beginning of considerable railway development in the area, and by which time Preston's industrial base was well established. The new railway reduced the time taken by stagecoach from three hours to less than half an hour. The inaugural return trip from Preston to Wigan was duly reported on in the *Preston Chronicle*: 'Loud huzzas greeted our arrival, the bells sent forth their sonorous peals, the Union Jack was unfurled on the Parish church, the standard of St. George floated on top of the Mayor's Mansion and a band of music played in the gardens'. The Wigan & Preston Junction Railway became part of the North Union Railway on 1 November 1838.

The original station of 1838 comprised of only two platforms, which had expanded to six tracks, four platforms and an extended station building by 1847. The Preston historian, A. Hewitson, writing in 1883, did not speak too favourably about the original North Union Station or of the first steam engines: 'At Preston the station was one of the most dismal, dilapidated, disgraceful-looking structures in Christendom. It was not only a very ill-looking, but an exceedingly inconvenient dangerous station... Often, when a heavy train was leaving Preston for the north, porters had to push at the side by way of giving them assistance'. [5]

Passengers had to cross the railway lines to reach other platforms, although this dangerous procedure was finally ended when a footbridge was erected in 1855. Increased volume of traffic and the appalling lack of facilities on the original station led to the construction of a more substantial structure, which was completed by the firm of Cooper and Tullis in July 1880. Further extensions were made in 1903 and 1913, when Preston Station reached its zenith with a total of fifteen platforms inclusive of bays. At the time it was said to be one of the finest in existence and, significantly, the original Platform 2, was signalled for use, either as an up or down line, and was often used by Longridge-bound trains.

Preston's Victorian railway network originally had five stations operated by rival companies. The evolving railway network was assisted by the inadequacy of the road system and the high profits made by the canal operators. Iron rails for horse-drawn wagons were used extensively during the second half of the eighteenth century and, therefore, the construction of the PLR followed a similar pattern. In fact, at the time of construction it was stated: 'That of all the railway undertakings now progressing the PLR may be considered as passing the greatest novelty and fairest proposal of emolument to those who have embarked their capital in the scheme and that has superior advantages over any line we have heard of. The country between Preston and Longridge is so remarkably favourable to give a preponderance of gravity to within three quarters of a mile of Preston. In addition to Longridge stone, lime from Chipping will be conveyed upon the railway after being carted from the kilns to the station at Newtown.' (Longridge) [6]

The Preston to Longridge branch line was originally completed in 1839, being only second in the order of railways to open around Preston, on May Day, 1840. However, at first the six and a half mile long railway emerged as a relatively obscure, self-contained branch line, originally detached from any other railway line and therefore not part of the evolving railway network. The Lancaster and Preston Junction Railway (L&PJR) opened on 25 June 1840; the original terminus at Preston being situated a short distance from the North Union Station, on the north side of Fishergate. The company painted their carriages in bright yellow and bestowed individual names upon them, as with the stagecoaches of yesteryear and the luxury Pullman carriages of a later era. The Lancaster & Carlisle Railway extended the line over Shap, to reach Carlisle in 1846 and Glasgow in 1848, although before that time an important route to Scotland was via the Fleetwood–Ardrossan Ferry.

On 15 July 1840, the Preston & Wyre Railway was opened, connecting Preston with Fleetwood, with ambitious plans for the development of Fleetwood as a port. Before the Furness Railway was established in 1862, the Lake District and the earliest fragmented railway around Morecambe bay was served by a paddle-steamer operating from Fleetwood to Bardsea, near Ulverston. It was advertised as 'A fine steamer, the quickest, cheapest and most agreeable route to the lakes and other attractions of the beautiful district'. [7] Later branch lines to Blackpool would establish both Blackpool and Fleetwood as popular seaside resorts by the late Victorian era. Apart from the significance of the port of Fleetwood for passenger and commercial traffic, the PWR was one of the first to run cheap excursion trains, the passengers being conveyed in open carriages from Preston to Fleetwood for about two shillings return. The PWR terminus station at Preston opened at Maudland on 16 July 1840, and was situated east of the L & PJR and north-east of the main North Union station, with access from Leighton Street. Nearby the PWR engine shed stabled up to six locomotives.

Train access to and from the original PWR Maudland Station involved a particularly hazardous crossing on the level by a double track over the L&PJR line. An accident occurred on 18 December 1840, when a PWR train collided with a ballast train on the Lancaster line and a railway worker was killed. Therefore, in February 1844 the PWR passenger traffic was transferred to the

This goods warehouse occupied the site of the original PWR Station at Maudland; behind is the elegant spire of St Walburge's Church. Courtesy: David Eaves

The map illustrates the first railways around Preston and features the Preston to Wyre line (top) and its Maudland terminus as well as the FP&WRR extension through the Maudland tunnel.

North Union Station and Maudland Station became closed to regular passenger traffic, although not to goods and excursion traffic bound for the Lancashire seaside resorts. The crossing continued to be a source of trouble and several more accidents occurred prior to its complete removal in 1885. On 18 September 1845, an up train from Lancaster severed a Fleetwood-bound excursion train of thirty trucks tightly packed with day-trippers. Miraculously, no one was killed, although many passengers sustained serious injuries. On 16 March 1847, a P&W engine left its shed at Maudland and collided with a train of cattle wagons on an up train from Lancaster. Both engines were badly damaged, but the crews escaped serious injury by climbing onto the tenders.

In the meantime, the Preston to Blackburn line opened in May 1846, with coaching stock painted in a blue and black livery. The East Lancashire Railway's line was accessed from Preston Station's eastern, or Butler Street, entrance and was served by its own platforms adjacent to the main North Union Station. The amalgamation of the ELR with the Lancashire & Yorkshire Railway took place on 13 August 1859. The Butler Street Station, then constituted L&YR property and was owned and operated solely by the L&YR for trains approaching Preston along their own independent route from the south-east via a station called Preston Junction, later to be known as Todd Lane Junction.

In October 1846, a branch was constructed from the main station to serve the Victoria Quay on the River Ribble, via a steep gradient of 1 in 29. The line was extended to serve the new Preston Docks in 1882. Following the closure of the docks in 1981, the line continues to be used for commercial freight and is also operated in part by the Ribble Steam Railway as a splendid 1¾ mile long heritage line.

The final major railway construction project in the Preston area was the West Lancashire Railway route from Fishergate Hill to Southport via Hesketh Bank, this opening on 15 September, 1882. The original terminus at Fishergate Hill was closed in 1900 to passengers after only eighteen years when the Lancashire & Yorkshire Railway, who had just absorbed the Company, extended the line to their Butler Street terminus.

With the expansion of the network, better facilities were needed for the servicing and stabling of locomotives, and engine-sheds were built to serve the railways entering Preston. The North Union's depot was originally situated at Butler Street, to the east of the main line. Ordnance Survey maps show that the East Lancashire Railway/L&YR was situated in the angle of the junction east of the main line and possessed its own engine-shed, with up to five roads, capable of stabling around twenty locomotives. This shed was the forerunner of Lostock Hall shed, opened by the L&YR in 1882.

The Lancaster & Preston Junction's shed was built on the west side of Maudland Junction and by 1850 had eight roads and a turntable. The Lancaster & Carlisle Railway Company built a new shed at the same location in 1857, this later being used in succession by the LNWR, LMS and British Railways.

Lostock Hall continued as a working depot until the end of steam in August 1968, thereby eclipsing Preston shed, which closed as a result of a disastrous fire occurring on 28 June 1960. Long before that, Preston shed prevailed at a time when Britain's passenger railways grew to 13,500 miles of track by 1870, rising to over 20,000 miles, operated by some 120 competing companies by the time of the First World War. The Preston historian, Hewitson noted in 1883: 'As to railways, Preston has, for many years, been one of the principal centres ... No town in the Kingdom possesses a more comprehensive railway service ... Prestonians possess facilities which but few provincial people, enjoy anywhere. About 450 trains passenger and goods arrive at and depart from the principal station every twenty four hours'. [8]

Since those golden years of the railways and lamentably, perhaps due to a lack of vision, the somewhat modest Longridge branch line and several other branch lines emanating from Preston have now passed into the annals of railway history. In that the PLR was ever constructed in the first place, we owe a debt of gratitude to the men of foresight who built the railways and thus provided vital links to the outside world prompting a social revolution, which impacted on local communities throughout the country. In successive chapters we will see that, corresponding with the growth of Lancashire's railway network, the PLR nevertheless ranks as a significant nineteenth century development, especially for the crucial Longridge quarrying industry and the local communities that the passenger service served, at Deepdale (Preston) Ribbleton, Grimsargh and Longridge.

From Equine Quadruped to Iron Horse

Chapter Two examines the formation of the Preston & Longridge Railway Company and the construction of the line, while analysing its social and economic impact between the official openings on May Day 1840 and the time when it was leased to a new consortium in 1846, known as the Fleetwood, Preston & West Riding Junction Railway Company.

The PLR Company was conceived in 1835 several years prior to the beginnings of the national railway network, when a provisional committee comprising the Chairman, Peter Hesketh Fleetwood (also Chairman of the Preston & Wyre Railway and MP for Preston), along with five other local directors, James Blanchard, James Dilworth, Charles Buck, David Nuttall and James Fair, produced a prospectus to establish the financial implications of the formation of the railway company. The prospectus alluded to the expansion of Preston and to benefits over road transport for the Longridge quarrying industry. For example, 'Two horses, with great labour, draw three tons per day on the road, while, on the railway they would be able to pull 40 tons with much less difficulty'.

The company's capital of £30,000 was divided into 600 shares of £50 each. It was estimated that the line would cost £30,000 to build with costs comprising: land £4,000, cuttings and embankments £6,000, ballast £1,950, track materials £10,000, bridges £1,050, fencing, gates and drainage £2,150, cranes and buildings £1,700, horses and wagons £1,000 and legal expenses £1,000. Sub total £28,050. Add Contingencies £1950: Total £30,000. This would yield a profit of 15 per cent per annum on the volume of stone traffic alone, while passenger receipts were not even taken into account. It was expected that the annual return would be £6,633. [9]

There was opposition to the first railways from those engaged in certain rival transport systems. In addition, owners of farmland were concerned about the intrusion of railways onto their land and the dangers caused to cattle grazing in fields adjoining railway property. Nevertheless, the PLR Company was incorporated under Acts 6–7 William IV and was given the Royal assent on 14

July 1836, authorising construction of the line from Preston to the entrance of the Tootle Heights complex of quarries at the western end of Longridge Fell.

The legislators specified that the line was to be horse-worked and could carry stone, passengers and all kinds of goods. The toll for every horse, mule, ass, ox, cow, bull or meat cattle was three pence a mile, calf or pig 1½ pence per mile, sheep or lamb a penny and a parcel weighing less than a ton, sixpence a mile. The company should not charge less than 1/- per ton for short distances. No locomotive or fixed engine was to be used without the consent of two Justices of the Peace. It transpired that steam power was not used on the line until eight years after the official opening. It was also stipulated that the railway was not to pass Grimsargh with Brockholes chapel on the southern side (the extant St Michael's Church) or pass within 100 yards of the House of Recovery, which later came to be known as the Preston Royal Infirmary. Significantly, although the prospectus had only referred to the carriage of stone, the Act of Parliament clearly specified that the line could carry passengers and all kinds of goods.

By 1836, the PLR management had been reconstituted under the chairmanship of Thomas Batty Addison, who was the Recorder of Preston and Tory opponent of the famous Liberal and advocate of temperance, Joseph Livesey. A meeting of twelve shareholders/directors was convened at Preston Town Hall on 9 September 1836, with the following present: Thomas B. Addison (Chairman), James Blanchard, John Winstanley, Philip Parke, Charles Buck, John Cunliffe, Thomas Birchall, William Talbot, Robert Friend, Richard Walmsley, Isaac Wilcockson and Joseph Bray, along with James Dixon (Solicitor) and James Webster (Secretary). [10] According to a local Preston Trade Directory, the mood was upbeat about the future prosperity of the line: 'We hope that the spirited proprietors will form themselves into a trading company for the conveyance of stone, limestone from the kilns and quarries near Longridge; and the transit of corn and other commodities from Preston to Clitheroe and other parts. But to ensure success cheapness must be the order of the day'.

A survey was undertaken and maps drawn indicating the route from St Paul's Square, Preston, to Tootle Heights Quarry, Longridge. Construction commenced under the secretary-ship of Alexander Bannerman. It transpired that the original Preston terminus of the branch was not St Paul's Square, but was in fact a station situated on Deepdale Street, east of Deepdale Road, and which has now been demolished. The Company engaged Mr H. Bushell, a resident civil engineer, to supervise the entire project and tenders for construction of the line were invited and advertised in the *Preston Chronicle* during January 1838. Excavations, earthworks and track laying were contracted to a Mr Wilkie. Messrs. Cooper and Tullis built several of the bridges and the single-line tunnel leading to the quarries. In April 1838, it was reported that the directors were in little doubt that the whole work would be finished by the end of the year. It was expected that the contractors would be able to finish the earthworks, culverts and bridges and increase their workforce, by employing 'handloom weavers who are out of work and barely able to obtain food'. [11]

This reference to the plight of the handloom weavers in 1840 mirrors the conditions in Victorian Preston, when the town clearly witnessed considerable strife, unemployment and poverty. Progress on the line's construction was slow. According to the *Preston Chronicle* the 'principal reasons why completion has been so long delayed, are the diversion of the line from the originally intended direction, (a reference to site transfer of Preston terminus from St Paul's Square to Deepdale Street) the extreme wetness of the weather for the last two seasons and that, at Longridge, a tunnel had to be constructed in order that the line could enter the most productive quarries'. [12]

There is little evidence as to what the original gauge of the PLR may have been, as at first there was no legal compulsion for standard gauge and, during the nineteenth century, there were three different gauges in use by the various railway companies. However, with the inauguration of steam locomotion in 1848, the rails would almost certainly have conformed to the statutory requirements of the Gauge Act, 1846, as a 4 ft 8½ in standard-gauge line. It was constructed as a single-track line with rails set onto 18 in square stone sleepers by means of two wooden pegs. These first sleepers were made from blocks of stone quarried in

Rails were set onto 18-inch square stone sleepers by means of two wooden pegs, as can be seen in this photograph. Courtesy: George Whiteman Collection

Longridge but, according to Hewitson, 'stone sleepers in combination with poor quality metals made rail travel, even in the 1st class carriages, an experience to be endured'.

The Victorian historian and author of *A History of Longridge*, Tom Smith, was later to applaud Victorian enterprise on the Longridge line: 'A very useful invention for curbing the screws, (to tighten the metals) was made by the late Mr William Banks. Before his invention, the price charged for curbing was from 8/- to 4/-, whereas Mr Banks contracted for the work on the Longridge line at 2/- a metal. Notwithstanding the great reduction in price, Mr Banks was able to make as much as £8 a day. Within twelve months his plan was in use on all the railway lines in the Kingdom; and his patent was sold for only £5'. [13]

The original plan of the PLR indicates a basic railway, with a single short quarry extension at Longridge. As the quarrying industry expanded, so did the Railway and a second single-line extension to the PLR was opened to the Lord Derby (or Lord's) Quarry by the end of the decade. [14] This quarry proved productive, employing up to seventy men, who were greatly assisted by the provision of a narrow-gauge railway that brought the stone down for loading into trucks in a private siding. The upper line extension was constructed to serve the largest workings at the Tootle Heights complex of five quarries.

From the junction, the route curved on a gradient of 1 in 30, to a tunnel entrance leading directly into the most productive quarries. There was a short section of double-track, with sidings and stabling for the horses, which reduced to single-track at the entrance to the extant fifty yard single bore tunnel that led direct into 'railway quarry'. On reaching the tunnel, with height restrictions of only 13 feet from the level of the standard-gauge line, the wagons were winched by rope

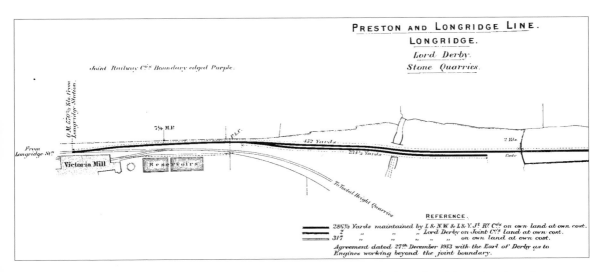

At Longridge, the extended railway led to Lord Derby Quarry on the lower line. The point where the upper line diverged to Tootle Heights was at Victoria Mill. Courtesy: Mike Atherton Collection

The upper line extension leading towards the tunnel at Tootle Heights, just before the commencement of double-track; centre is the solitary chimney at Lord Derby's Quarry, served by the Lower Line. Courtesy: George Whiteman Collection

The commencement of double-track on the upper line. At this point, the line crossed over a road that led to Willow Farm. Courtesy: George Whiteman Collection

The double-track section of the upper line, complete with switch points, looking towards Longridge Station. Courtesy: George Whiteman Collection

The quarry tunnel and weigh-bridge (foreground). The tracks leading to the quarries were lifted around 1940. Courtesy: Longridge & District Local History Society

The remains of the loading dock situated along the weigh-bridge outside the tunnel entrance to the quarries. Courtesy: George Whiteman Collection

The remains of the quarry lines, showing the upper and lower line bridges, c. 1959. Courtesy: Longridge & District Local History Society

The extant lower quarry line bridge, photographed in 2009. Courtesy: Robert Gregson

All that remains of Lord's Delph quarry (right) at the end of the lower line. The photograph, taken in 2008, illustrates Billington's and the picturesque countryside looking north towards the Bowland fells. David Hindle

Above: The author outside the entrance to the 50-yard long tunnel that led direct into the Tootle Height complex of quarries. The portal to the blocked-off tunnel under Higher Road is a Grade II listed building. Courtesy: Robert Gregson

Left: The restored keystone above the tunnel entrance chronicles some interesting facts: the letters P&LR signify Preston & Longridge Railway; '1839' is the date of completion; C&T to Cooper and Tullis, the builders; while the initials FHP are said to relate to engineer Frederick Henry Park. It has also been suggested that these initials may be an anagram of the original Chairman, Peter Hesketh Fleetwood (back to front). Courtesy: Robert Gregson

using a crane in the quarry to pull the trucks through the tunnel for loading with stone. Extensive sidings were established in the quarry and, once loaded, gravity facilitated the trucks being pushed back through the tunnel to a weighbridge and loading wharf, situated at the north side of the tunnel. Stone was brought from several quarries that could not be reached by rail to the loading wharf, where there was also a crane for lifting the dressed stone into waiting wagons.

In anticipation of the official opening of the railway, the *Preston Pilot* newspaper carried an advertisement mentioning the facilities for letting at Deepdale. The earliest available working timetable preceded the opening of the railway and was advertised in the *Preston Chronicle* on 25 April 1840: 'A carriage for conveyance of passengers will leave Preston for Longridge every Wednesday and Saturday morning at half past seven o'clock and return from Longridge at half past eight o'clock. In the afternoon it will leave Preston at four o'clock and return from Longridge at five o'clock.' [15]

The Chairman, Thomas Batty Addison, officially opened the line linking Preston Deepdale Street with Longridge on 1 May 1840. On this auspicious occasion a large party, including several directors, assembled at the Preston terminus at ten o'clock precisely, along with villagers, to cheer the inaugural passenger train drawn by a horse decorated with ribbons. With the official opening for the conveyance of stone and passengers, came an altogether cleaner environment. Addison stipulated that the railway would be horse-worked until the full working potential could be ascertained and then steam traction would be considered.

This description of the route from a local trade directory describes the particular features along the line from Longridge to Preston: 'The line of the railway commences at its eastern extremity, in a field on the western part of an estate near Longridge, lately purchased by the railway company, situated in the township of Dilworth, and is about two hundred yards from the high road leading from many of the trading towns in the eastern parts of Lancashire and Yorkshire to Preston. At Tootle Heights, Longridge, the railway is cut out of solid rock. There is a fine view of the Chipping Hills and the diversified scenery, which adorns the landscape below. Further west it proceeds towards the Plough Inn, in Grimsargh, which it passes within 10 yards and is then carried in a straight line to the eastern part of the 'Parsonage House' in Grimsargh, and to the south is the antique residence of Mrs Cross, called The Red Scar House. In this direction another bridge occurs, of wood, under which the line is constructed. It then passes the garden of the School House, and thence, without any material angle or curve, proceeds under another bridge (Gamull Lane) near to Ribbleton Brow; thence it proceeds in a regular direction to the terminus near to Barton Terrace.' [16]

The first passenger stations on the PLR were decidedly crude, being situated at Deepdale Street, Grimsargh and Longridge. The earliest station at Longridge was situated next to the main street and level crossing at Burey Lane – later called Berry Lane – in what was then a small village. Indeed, before Longridge Station was built in 1872 as an adjunct to the extant Towneley Arms Hotel, only rudimentary platform facilities were provided. [17] It was only after the railway was converted to steam power in 1848 and the industrial revolution had made its impact, that a rapid expansion of Longridge was triggered. A timetable of sorts was implemented as the railway came into full operation, primarily as a mineral line, although most trains were mixed, carrying both passengers and heavy stone.

More permanent stations were not built for some years and, indeed, Deepdale Street Station bore the date inscription 1850, suggesting that the building was not the original one. The station was a two-storey building with a central passage that led from Deepdale Street to the platform area. Deepdale Street Station should not be confused with a station bearing the name Deepdale Bridge, which opened about a mile away on the new line of the Fleetwood, Preston & West Riding Junction Railway (as described in Chapter Three).

The original intermediate station of Grimsargh utilised a downstairs room of the Plough Inn as the booking office, for an annual rent of 20 shillings. The single platform is shown on old maps to have been adjacent to the inn. Those who rode into Grimsargh to continue their journey by train used the Plough stables as a Victorian equivalent of a 'park-and-ride'. The 1841 census shows Mary and William Walmsley as mine hosts and six family members whose ages ranged

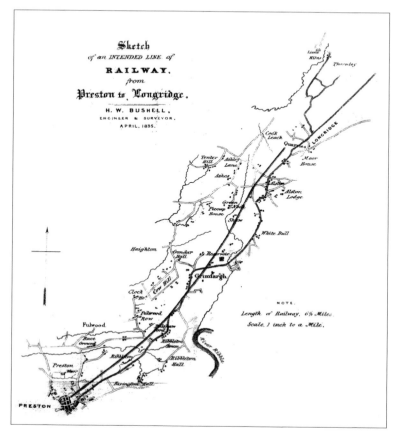

Original 1835 map, showing the course of the Preston to Longridge Railway. Courtesy: Harris Reference Library

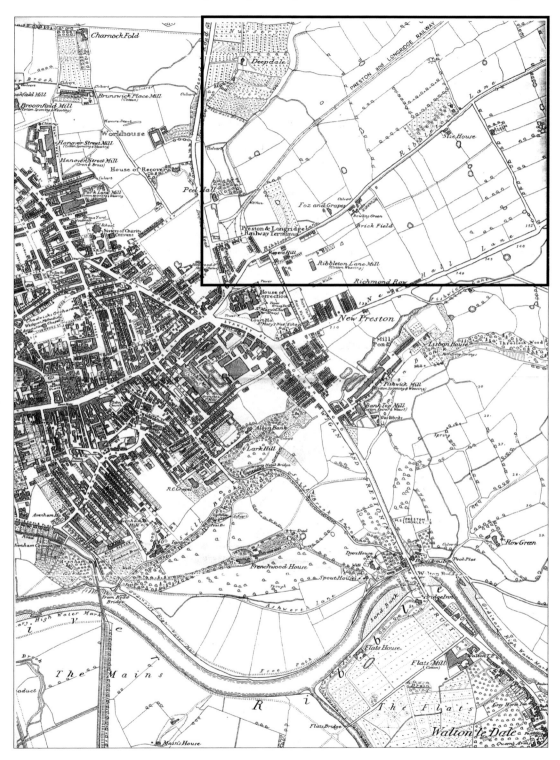

Map showing the original terminus of the station in Deepdale Street, Preston and its isolation from the emerging railway network. Courtesy: Peter Adams, Heritage Cartography

The Plough Inn, Grimsargh, was at first used as a combined pub and railway station. The section of the building on the left was the booking office and had a platform adjacent thereto. Courtesy: Tom Heginbotham

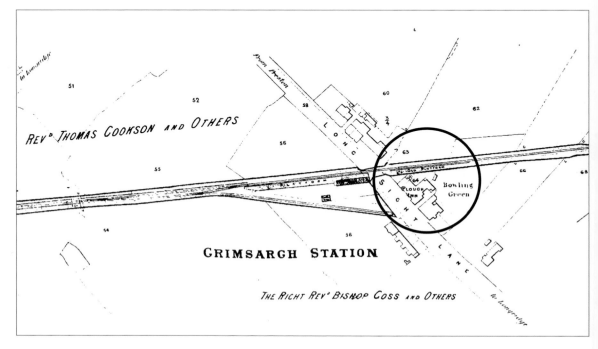

The original Grimsargh Station is shown on this plan to have a platform adjacent to the Plough Inn on Long Sight Lane. Courtesy: Tom Heginbotham

Deepdale Street Station was the original Preston terminus of the Longridge railway and the town's second railway station but, alas, now demolished. Courtesy: Stephen Sartin

A 1966 view of the course of the branch between Longridge and Grimsargh Stations, looking south from the occupation crossing at Shay Lane. Courtesy: George Whiteman Collection

from four to twenty-four years. Some passengers may even have treated the first
stationmaster, George Bleasdale, to a pint or enjoyed a game of bowls with him
when he finished his shift. [18] For the record, it is known that Howard Latham
was stationmaster at Grimsargh in 1853 [19] and, by 1892 it was a certain Richard
Potts. [20] By 1926, Howard Latham's namesake descendant 'kept it in the family'
by assuming the stationmaster position [21] and where he remained until the last
passenger train departed from Grimsargh Station on 2 June 1930.

The passenger service appears to have been extremely popular for, within a
few weeks of the opening of the line in 1840, the *Preston Chronicle* carried a
letter from a correspondent using the nom de plume 'Confined Artisan', and
requesting the railway company to provide a Sunday service, as 'the railway
provided a little recreation in the country on the Sabbath day'. The service
was increased by 1841, to implement Sunday workings: two conveyances for
passengers ran between Preston and Longridge on Sundays, Wednesdays and
Saturdays. The fare from Preston to the Plough Inn at Grimsargh was 4d and to
Longridge 6d. [22]

Departures from Preston to Longridge	Departures from Longridge to Preston
7am and 3pm Wednesday	9.30am and 6pm Wednesday,
7am and 4pm Saturday	8am and 6pm Saturday
8am and 2pm Sunday	9.15am and 6pm Sunday

It was not until the coming of steam traction in 1848 that there were daily
services on weekdays, with more trains on Sundays. The *Preston Chronicle*
alludes to both the passenger carriages and to the number of horses required for
their conveyance at the time of the opening of the line, although passengers were
permitted to ride on the stone wagons if they so desired: 'Two of the carriages
have been have been constructed on a peculiar principal for the special purposes
of this railway, and which are adapted either for passengers or luggage of any
description, were put in readiness, and horses, ornamented and caparisoned after
the usual style of the 1st May, were yoked to them, three to the first carriage,
and two the second.' [23]

It seems likely that initially these conveyances were 3rd class open carriages. It
was the Railway Regulation Act, 1844, that required all companies to provide at
least one train a day consisting of 3rd class covered accommodation, travelling
at not less than twelve miles per hour, for which the rate was not to exceed 1d
a mile. Nevertheless, as late as 1868, passengers were still travelling in open
3rd class carriages and consequently, being exposed to the elements, took their
umbrellas with them.

Victorian safety on the PLR parallels archetypal incidents throughout the
country. The diversity of accident causes ranged from jumping or falling off

wagons and brake and signal failure, to animals and inebriated men on the tracks. A contemporary leaflet, 'Rules for Railway Travelling' provided general advice to the first Victorian travellers: 'If a 2nd class carriage, as sometimes happens, has no door passengers should take care not to put out their legs. Beware of yielding to a sudden impulse to spring from the carriage to recover your hat, which has blown off, or a parcel that has been dropped'. Hewitson refers to an incident on the PLR when a boy travelling in one of the open carriages lost his cap between Grimsargh and Longridge. 'The train was stopped in order that a lad might recover his cap. After this young passenger recovered his hat preparations were made for restarting the train but the carriages had lost their momentum and so one or more horses lower down the line had to be sent for before the journey continued.' [24]

From Longridge, loaded wagons with over 100 tons of stone went downhill under their own gravity towards Preston with a brakeman/engineer in charge. According to Hewitson, 'Many a time when the wind was blowing strongly in the rear, trains ran for some distance past the stopping place in Grimsargh.' [25] The horses were attached to the wagons for the final haul into Preston. During this initial period of horse-drawn operation, they hauled well over 1,000 tons of stone per week from Longridge for processing at Deepdale. This represented a considerable increase over the road-haulage traffic that took place before the line was built.

The first serious accident on the line occurred in January 1846, and involved a quarry worker, William Crook, who was returning from Longridge to Preston with two other men. All three individuals were seated at the front of a stone wagon, but, at Ribbleton, the stone gave way and Crook fell onto the lines, trapping his leg under the stone. A wagon wheel then crushed the limb before the wagon could be stopped. 'After being extricated, he was brought on to the Ribbleton Bowling Green public house, and Mr. Booth, a local surgeon, was immediately called in, who, after examining the limb, declared at once the absolute necessity of an immediate amputation, which was complied with and successfully performed.' [26]

From Hedonism to Employment Opportunities

The primitive Longridge branch line began to impact on the lives of the first railway passengers and transports of delight were augmented at holiday time, whenever the necessary horsepower was available. As early as Whitsuntide 1840, the PLR proved to be popular with the public (especially on public holidays), who could now explore Longridge Fell and the Ribble Valley, thus escaping from the grime and poverty of Preston's Industrial Revolution: 'We noticed that the Directors arranged extra trains on Whit Monday. Parties availed themselves of quick transport to and from the upper end of the line. Others went by early trains for a day's ramble on the hills to enjoy the beautiful and almost unlimited variety of scenery, which presents itself from the heights above Longridge, there being no less than 418 conveyed along the line. Some trains came down the steepest part of the incline at nearly 40 m.p.h.' [27]

During Whit Monday, 1841, the horse-drawn trains, running in both directions, evidently enhanced the lives of passengers boarding at Preston, Grimsargh and Longridge. The delights of newly-found holiday travel continued with increasing momentum, enabling Prestonians to discover the Longridge countryside and the curiosities of the new railway: 'Among the various ways of spending the holiday there has not been a more rational one proposed that that of a trip to the beautiful heights of Longridge from whence, should the weather prove good, the view of wood and water can be enjoyed, embracing as it does an immense extent of country bounded in the far distance by the sea. The facilities have been much increased since the opening of the Preston-Longridge railway. The journey home has something of a novelty if we consider that the rate is from twenty to thirty miles per hour, without the aid of horse or steam.' [28]

The cultural and social interests of rural villagers were also met, with pleasure-seeking trips to Preston. Here they would witness brass bands and contemporary temperance processions, whilst perhaps seeking advice from the friendly societies, which met in pubs and would often be available to negotiate funds for sickness and unemployment: 'Three hundred and fifty seven passengers were conveyed on the Preston to Longridge Railway, with four trains despatched each way to explore the fells and quarries of Longridge, and the good folk had a chance to witness the festivities of Preston on Whit Monday. This included the Friendly Societies paraded in the mornings and the Temperance Society paraded in the afternoon, both with bands of music. In the thronged streets, itinerant musicians from a blind fiddler attended only by his dog, to a complete band of first rate performers were exerting themselves to the seekers of pleasure.' [29]

Certain hedonistic activities were doubtless sought in pub concert rooms and other dubious establishments for the 'seekers of pleasure.' A reference to the level of prostitution in Victorian Preston in the *Chronicle* confirmed that 'Friargate was infested by bonnet-less young girls and something ought to be done about the 120 women and girls known to the police as being on the streets of Preston'. For those that could afford it, there was the conviviality of the pub, where the drink trade doubtless provided some solace, although hardly a level of sobriety, despite the proactive temperance campaigns. In Preston, throughout the nineteenth century, there was an abundance of public houses and beer shops that peaked at around 490 such premises during the 1870s.

With the introduction of the railway, people were more mobile and migration from rural areas to the urban environment of Preston was extensive for those seeking regular employment and better wages in the dominant textile industry and other trades. The development of the railway network from 1838 had a part to play in the growth of the music hall – first established in public house concert rooms. The place of Preston at the forefront of national music hall growth

Longridge stone was used in the construction of the Sessions House (left) and Harris Museum, Preston. Courtesy: Longridge & District Local History Society

is illustrated by the pioneering, although decadent, 'Albion Singing Saloon', Clarke's Yard, Church Street, which opened in 1839, the same year that the PLR was completed.

Recreational activities such as these probably provided a diversion from the blood, sweat and tears of the original quarrymen. Their hard work is mirrored throughout north-west England. Bolton Parish Church, Blackpool Promenades and Liverpool Docks all have their origins in Longridge stone. At Preston, buildings constructed of ashlar stone include the Minster, St Walburge's Church, Fishergate Baptist Church, the Harris Museum, Preston Railway Station, Fulwood Barracks and Preston Docks.

However, despite the contribution of the railway to a social comfort and the lavishness of some of Preston's finest buildings, it nevertheless endured mixed economic fortunes. During the first six years of operation, profits fell short of the anticipated fifteen per cent dividends per annum, with no dividend paid to the shareholders, prompting the directors to consider the future of the line and the possibility of a takeover by another company.

CHAPTER THREE

The line that never was

The First Stage of Railway Mania

This chapter examines the period of Fleetwood, Preston & West Riding Junction Railway ownership and their grandiose plans for the PLR in 1846, until take-over by the Joint London & North Western and Lancashire & Yorkshire Railway Company on 17 July 1867.

Owing to the precarious financial state of the PLR in 1846, after only six years of operation, an outright sale to the Preston & Wyre Railway Company was duly considered and rejected. Instead, the PWR Company sponsored the formation of a new consortium, the Fleetwood, Preston & West Riding Junction Railway Company, (FP&WRJR) which formed an alliance with the PLR Company and from whom they leased the railway. The newly-formed company, chaired by Mr Thomas Addison, sought powers to play a key role in the railway mania years of 1846/47, when over one thousand miles of line were added to Britain's railway network. Their ambitious plans were to promote the commercial viability of the port of Fleetwood with the profitable traffic of a new railway linking Fleetwood with the cities of Leeds and Hull. Equally, it would give people on the other side of the Pennines access to the seaside resorts of Fleetwood and Blackpool. Moreover, the eloquence of the gracious age of Victorian respectability expressed its objective as to 'facilitate intercourse between the West Riding and the Colonies, via Fleetwood'.

The cumbersome title 'Fleetwood, Preston & West Riding Junction Railway,' broadly reflected the proposed route from Fleetwood via Preston and the Preston & Longridge Railway with the planned Blackburn, Clitheroe & North West Junction Railway (BC&NWJR) that was to link Blackburn, via Clitheroe and Chatburn, to a junction at Elslack on the Skipton to Colne line in West Yorkshire. New railways were also proposed, linking Mitton near Whalley to Burnley and East Lancashire and from Chatburn to Long Preston. History shows that none of these specific links were to reach their original intended destinations.

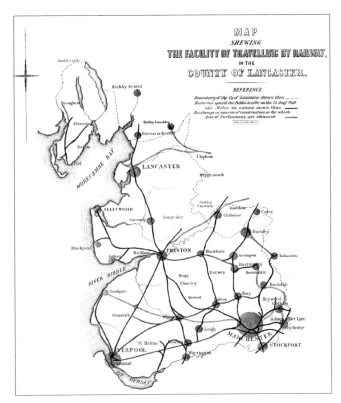

Right: Map of 1861, showing the first railways of Lancashire and featuring the proposed course of the Fleetwood, Preston & West Riding Junction Railway. It was originally proposed that the route of this railway would branch off the PLR at Grimsargh and go via Clitheror to Elslack (south of Skipton). Courtesy: Harris Reference Library

Below: Map illustrating the Blackburn, Clitheroe and North West Junction Railway (right) and its proximity to the short PLR (centre)

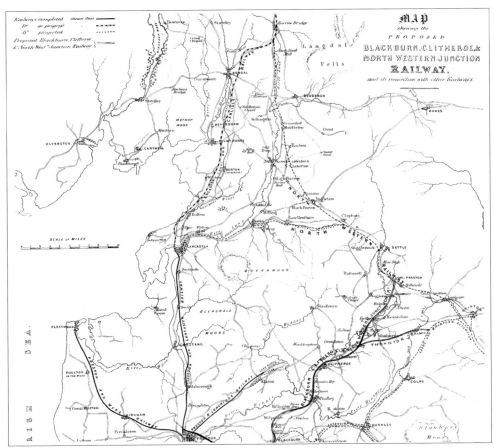

The isolation of the Longridge line foresaw the need for a link with the emerging railway network. Crucial to the route proposed by the Fleetwood Company was the construction of a connecting railway of one mile 406 yards, linking Maudland with the PLR at Deepdale Junction. From Deepdale, three miles of the middle section of the original Longridge line were to be utilised, up to a digression point situated south of Grimsargh. A ten-mile link from Grimsargh was to be built, traversing the north bank of the River Ribble, passing through the parishes of Grimsargh with Brockholes, Elston, Alston with Hothersall, Ribchester, Stidd, Dutton, Dilworth, Mitton, Bailey with Chaigley, Dinckley, Salesbury, Billington, Whalley, and Pendleton, before forming a junction with the proposed line from Blackburn to West Yorkshire. A contemporary report in the *Preston Pilot* extolled the virtues of the Ribblesdale project: 'In connection with the North East Railway, this line will also throw open the watering places of Harrogate and Knaresborough and the rich and beautiful scenery of Bolton Abbey and Wharfedale to the health and pleasure seeking denizens of Lancashire. In return the shores of Fleetwood, Blackpool and Lytham and the romantic district of the Lake County, will be brought within the easy reach of the population of Yorkshire and Durham. The lime beds in the vicinity of Clitheroe furnish the best quality of limestone in Lancashire, while the pastures of the Craven valley are the well-known resorts for the purpose of fattening for the markets of the manufacturing towns the cattle constantly imported from Ireland. The line will also afford great facility of access to the valuable stone quarries on the Longridge Fell, the purchase of which is included in the agreement for the Preston & Longridge Railway.' [30]

Conversely, opposition was expressed when interested parties were cross-examined on their views of a new railway that would cross the scenic Ribble Valley. There was resistance from local landowners and the principal of the prestigious Stonyhurst College, who expressed typical concerns of that period about the line destroying the picturesque features of a beautiful county. [31]

Nevertheless, the Fleetwood, Preston & West Riding Junction Railway Act of 1846 received the Royal Assent on 27 July 1846. Section 47 provided that power was given to demise, lease, sell, or otherwise dispose of the Preston & Longridge Railway Company to the Fleetwood Company. Sections 51 and 52 of the Act stated that, upon completion of the work, the Company was authorised to dispose of its undertaking to Preston & Wyre Railway Dock & Harbour Company, and thereafter the subsidiary Company was to be dissolved and wound up. The capital of the company constructing the line was £270,000, divided into 22,500 shares at £12 each. [32] The schedule provided a scale of tolls in respect of goods and passengers carried, and these are outlined in Appendix II. An agreement was signed for leasing the line for £3,000 per annum, payable to the PLR, and which came into effect on 1 January 1847.

The contract price for the link from Maudland Junction to Deepdale Junction was £69,000 and was to be undertaken by Mr George Mould, who was contracted to construct the Grimsargh to Clitheroe link for an undisclosed price.

Construction of the one mile Deepdale extension began with the cutting of the first sod, which took place on 18 January 1847 near to the 'House of Recovery' (the old Preston Royal Infirmary). To mark the event, the Mayor of Preston, John Paley, accompanied by the Mayor of Clitheroe, used an engraved silver spade and polished wheelbarrow. The spade bore the coat-of-arms of the County Palatine of Lancashire and the Boroughs of Preston and Clitheroe and was later presented to the Mayor of Preston. The barrow was of polished mahogany and bore the inscription, 'Fleetwood, Preston & West Riding Junction Railway – the first sod of this railway was cut on the Deepdale Road near Preston, by the Worshipful John Paley Junior, Esq., Mayor of Preston, 1847. The barrow used on this occasion by Thomas Batty Addison, Esq., Recorder of Preston and Chairman of the company, is presented to him in commemoration of the event by his brother Directors.' Addison proclaimed 'prosperity to the company' and remarked that 'the company could be sure to have their work well done if they gave as good ale as that to all their workmen. Amidst loud cheers, the distinguished guests enjoyed a customary meal, washed down with copious amounts of mulled ale.' [33]

At the sharp end of operations, the double-track route of the Preston link between Maudland and Deepdale junction necessitated 1,200 yards of cutting, a tunnel, five bridges over the line and a girder span bridge across the Preston to Kendal Canal. Messrs. Park and Bidder were appointed engineers and a survey revealed that the estimated constructional costs of the whole project

Share Certificate of the Fleetwood, Preston & West Riding Junction Railway. Courtesy: Robert Gregson

Engraving of the celebrations on 18 January 1847, at Deepdale, Preston. Courtesy: Robert Gregson

This engraving marks the boundary of what was to become the Joint Line's property and was situated on the pavement at the corner of Deepdale Road and Burrow's Road. Courtesy: Gordon Biddle

would be in the region of £268,000. The Act contained a clause stating: 'The railway passing through the Borough of Preston shall pass under the streets and roads of the borough and not over or on a level with the said streets and roads.' In compliance with legal requirements, the route was tunnelled for 862 yards below the streets of the Borough of Preston. Originally, an open cutting was planned, but it transpired at a Company meeting in August 1847, that three sections of brick-lined tunnel would be built passing under Maudland Bank, St Peter's Square and North Road, emerging at Deepdale. Work on the Maudland tunnel, presented considerable engineering difficulties and was completed on 29 December 1849. Evidence of the importance of the proposed main line to West Yorkshire is apparent to this day, with earthworks at Ribbleton indicating that the railway had been constructed wide enough to take double tracks.

On 23 August 1847, an essential phase of the work commenced on the Ribble Valley project. About 15,000 cubic yards were excavated for a two hundred-metre railway cutting, sufficiently wide for double-track specification, between Clough Bank Wood and Bailey Brook near Hurst Green. Substantial viaducts would have been required at either end to cross the deep wooded valleys and no building work took place. Twelve months later came premature curtailment of the extension through Ribblesdale. A bolt from the blue meant that the necessary engineering work was suspended, when the FP&WRJR Report for 1848 stated that 'although a certain amount of excavation work had been completed at Hurst Green, it was not proposed to proceed with the Clitheroe line, for the present'. Even more surprisingly, work came to an abrupt halt on the whole project, when it was revealed that the BC&NWJR would terminate at Chatburn, north of Clitheroe, instead of in West Yorkshire. However, in 1879 the L&YR absorbed the Blackburn undertaking and extended the line from Chatburn to a junction at Hellifield with the now famous Settle to Carlisle line, which was completed in 1875.

Consequently, the original plan to extend to Elslack was abandoned. There was disquiet among the shareholders of the FP&WRR at a meeting held on 28 February 1849, when it was announced that all work on the extension from Grimsargh would be terminated. Several issues caused alarm and frustrated their plans, these including the effective opposition of landowners and campaigns concerning the intrusion of the line into Ribblesdale. In addition, building work came into question, especially when the contractor, George Mould, had his budget reduced to £2,000 per month; it was then realised that the line was unlikely to reach West Yorkshire.

In 1888, Smith reflected on the opposition of landowners, while considering the original proposals worthwhile: 'The line was originally intended to be continued through Ribchester and Hurst Green to Yorkshire, but owing to the determined opposition of some of the then leading landowners in the district, the scheme was abandoned. It was a well-matured scheme, and it is a pity that such a splendid opportunity of developing this part of Lancashire should have failed through short-sighted opposition.' [34]

The railway cutting at Hurst Green proved to be the only substantial work carried out on the new link to Clitheroe. Over 170 years after construction, the earthworks still feature prominently in the serene landscape of Ribblesdale and are today frequented only by flocks of sheep. David Hindle

The one mile section that ran east of the main line from Maudland to the PLR at Deepdale Junction turned out to be the only section of track to be completed, and was opened for goods trains on 14 January 1850 and to passenger trains on 1 November 1856. An official 1851 entry in *Gillbank's Preston Directory* had cited grounds for superficial optimism with a Mr Richard Singleton, shown as Landlord of the then 'West Riding Railway Inn' that was formerly situated above the Maudland tunnel in North Street, Preston. Although the overall plans were to be permanently thwarted, its lasting legacy to this day is the curious folly of an excavated railway cutting nestling in the landscape of Ribblesdale.

At Hurst Green, a railway cutting of over 200 metres in length survives as a monument to this ill-fated Victorian enterprise. (Grid reference SD 682369). Nestling in splendid isolation the cutting is clearly recognisable as a detached and uncompleted portion of that once ambitious project, but beyond extending the line at Deepdale and constructing the Preston tunnel, they did little else but excavate this one field in Dutton. Had the line gone on, it would have traversed the lovely scenery of Ribblesdale. On either side, it is obvious that the steeply-wooded valleys would have necessitated the building of high viaducts. When I visited the site, I experienced a surreal encounter with this little-known, but nonetheless significant, railway landmark. While standing in the cutting, I took time to reflect upon its legacy, for there is something poignant about this place, which brings to mind the challenges, expectations and aspirations of the early Victorian railway speculators at the height of railway mania.

Steam Comes to Ribblesdale

Coinciding with the opening of a goods yard next to Berry Lane, the Chairman of the FP&WRJR, Thomas Batty Addison, introduced the first steam locomotive, appropriately named 'Addison', on Whit Monday, 12 June 1848, to replace the horse-drawn carriages that worked between Longridge and Deepdale Street. The permanent way was replaced with standard rails on transverse sleepers, although, because of the height restriction, the mineral wagons still had to be winched through the tunnel into the quarry and, from which, steam engines were excluded. The *Preston Chronicle* of 10 June 1848 duly advertised the inaugural steam passenger train: 'Cheap trains on Whit Monday and Tuesday, 12th and 18th June: the public are respectfully informed that a locomotive engine named "Addison" will be placed on the PLR, commencing on Monday the 12th instant for the conveyance of passengers.'

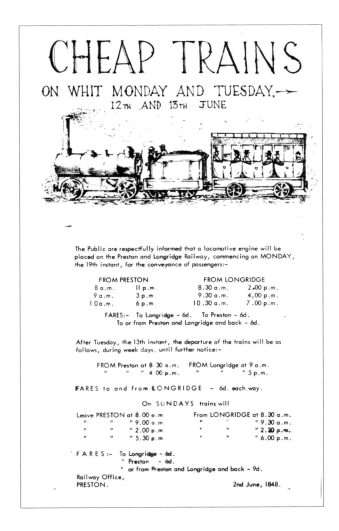

Advertisement in the *Preston Chronicle*, 10 June 1848, for the first steam run and special timetables and fares. No details are known of the original locomotive named 'Addison', although it is probable that the engine resembled the drawing depicted in the advert.

A *Preston Guardian* report mentioned the origins of the famed Longridge Brass Band, which originally consisted of scholars from Longridge Church of England school, who probably joined the band on leaving school. They witnessed the first steam engine to visit the town: 'The scholars walked in procession to the railway station enlivened by the school band to witness the starting of the steam engine'. [35]

The dawn of steam led to an increase to daily services on weekdays, with more trains on Sundays. The fare from Preston to Longridge was 6d each way and 9d return.

Departures from Preston to Longridge	Departures from Longridge to Preston
Weekdays: 8.30am and 4pm	Weekdays: 9am and 5pm
Sundays: 8am, 9am, 2pm and 5.30pm	Sundays: 8.30am, 9.30am, 2.30pm and 6pm

A further report described the ceremonial events of the day. [36] 'The officials of the railway company and a large party of officers from Fulwood Barracks were hauled by the engine, "Addison," along with some 200 invited guests and the band of the 89th from Deepdale Street, Preston, to Longridge terminus. However, the steep gradient to Longridge station proved too much for the esteemed locomotive and it ran out of steam. It therefore became necessary to split the train, with the locomotive taking the carriages up in two sections. A fairground had been set up at Tootle Heights and a dinner was laid on for the VIPs. After a speech by Thomas Addison, the Mayor of Preston gave a speech, when he poignantly urged the company to seek allegiance with the L&YR and LNWR.'

Twelve months later it became apparent that the Company could afford to purchase only additional 'well-used' locomotives and rolling stock. On 18 September 1849, at a total cost of £1,046, it acquired redundant second-hand stock from the Lancaster & Preston Railway, which had been forced to sell out to the Lancaster & Carlisle Railway. The sale comprised two Bury 2-2-0s locomotives with 5'6" driving wheels, named 'John 'O' Gaunt' and 'North Star' and possibly a third unknown engine of the same type, four coaches in green livery, eight carriage trucks, and seven goods vehicles. The new passenger carriages were painted green outside and yellow inside. Hewitson refers to them being 'painted in loud colours and bearing a particular name on the outside as the old horse-drawn coaches used to do'. (For full details of sale, see also Appendix III.)

Correspondingly, a class-conscious correspondent to the *Preston Guardian* wrote a contentious, although entertaining, letter about the sale of the redundant second-hand stock from the Lancaster & Preston Railway. From this, we can glean more revelations concerning this primitive railway and, in particular, that segregation of 1st, 2nd and 3rd Class had been implemented by 1849: 'I am informed on the best authority – a half brother of the stoker – that no less than four fresh carriages and two engines have been obtained ... The carriages are painted green outside and yellow inside, and have roofs, buffers and everything complete. They are to be divided into First, Second and Third-classes, so that plebeian and aristocratic passengers, may in future have their respective places, and that hideous system of republican equality or communism, which has hitherto prevailed on the Longridge line (and on some occasions has been carried so far as to lead to the admixture of bipeds and quadrupeds in the same carriage) will be done away with.' [37]

Judging by the tone of the correspondence, all was not well with management, while an engine-shed was now needed for 'Addison' and her second hand stable-mates. In complete contrast to the main Preston shed, the PLR was served by a humble one-road structure, with accommodation for two or three locomotives and was situated to the north of Deepdale Sidings near to the original station.

Additional transport resources led to the first excursion trains inducing passengers to reach far-flung destinations, even beyond Longridge, during Whitsuntide, 1851: 'Cheap excursions from Preston, by rail to the Towneley Arms, Longridge, where conveyances can be had for Whitewell and Chipping; 1s 6d 1st class, 1s 2nd class, and 6d 3rd class.' [38] Combined excursions such as this utilised a toast-rack like vehicle, known as a charabanc, enabling passengers to climb aboard. Each seat had its own door and the open-topped transport enabled passengers to discover and appreciate, in particular, the nearby Forest of Bowland, an area rich in history and scenic grandeur.

Bailiffs in Possession of Railway in 1852

By 1851, the company's finances were in a dire state, showing a meagre profit of £924. Despite a more regularised passenger service, the impact of the aborted plans to reach West Yorkshire had drained financial resources. The FP&WRR had not earned enough money to stay solvent, and could not even pay its rent of £3,000 per annum to the parent company, factors that led to bankruptcy in 1852. At the same time, the PWR discovered an 'escape-clause' in the wording of the 1846 legislation, which effectively meant a complete severance of their interest in the bankrupt company. The Preston & Longridge Company acquired the engines and rolling stock of the collapsed company, in lieu of owed rental fees, by means of a distress for rent auction sale took place at Longridge on 14 June 1852, when the stock of the FP&WRR was transferred to the PLR to recoup the rent. (See Appendix IV)

The events were so unusual as to warrant inclusion in the *Illustrated London News*: 'A circumstance perhaps unprecedented in railway annals has within the last few day occurred to the Preston to Longridge railway line, the result of which has been that the line has been unavoidably closed. The locomotive power, carriages and all the rolling stock have been taken into possession and sold under a warrant of execution ... The fortunes of the Fleetwood Preston & West Riding Junction Railway have turned out somewhat disastrous and their line in Yorkshire has not been carried out ... One consequence has been that the lessees have held rent from the lessors, who a few day ago, brought matters to a close by taking forcible possession of all the rolling stock, cranes and other equipment as well as all the office furniture, ticket machines & c. on all the various stations on the line. The stock was brought to the hammer on Monday. Whether the line will remain permanently closed will remain to be seen'. [39]

There followed protracted proceedings and the Preston & Longridge Railway Company legally commenced using the line on 15 November 1852, with the stock of the Fleetwood Preston & West Riding Junction Railway. Passenger services operated from 1840 to 1856 from the original Deepdale Street Station, with passengers being conveyed by carriage between the station and the main Preston Station, a distance of one mile. Despite the legal clauses for re-possession of the line, all trains were to terminate at Deepdale and none would run over the Fleetwood Preston & West Riding Junction Railway metals to Maudland Junction.

Re-possession and Improving Services in 1856

Stranger still, after being moribund for four years, the FP&WRR obtained powers to purchase the railway. Section 47 of a reincorporation act of 23 June 1856 authorised the sale to the newly reformed FP&WRR Company, with full and peaceable possession of the Preston & Longridge Railway and premises. The legislation largely repealed the Act of 1846. [40] It therefore transpired that the outright sale of the PLR to the FP&WRR was made for £48,000, payable in £6,000 instalments commencing 1 September 1856, the date upon which the reconstituted Company became the legal owner of the line.

On 1 November 1856, the Company introduced passenger services for the first time between Maudland and Longridge and the line through Maudland Tunnel was opened to passengers as well as freight, along with the two new stations on the extended line, at Maudland Bridge and Deepdale Bridge on Deepdale Road. The actual location of the new terminus (Maudland Bridge) was situated at the end of the deep stone-faced cutting, close to where the tracks crossed over the Lancaster Canal by an over-bridge and with access being afforded from Cold Bath Street. The opening coincided with a revised service to Longridge, with trains departing from Maudland Bridge Station at 8.30 a.m., 11 a.m., 3 p.m., and 6 p.m. and on Sundays at 9 a.m., 2.30 p.m. and 6 p.m. The return journey for 1st class passengers was 1s 9d and, for those passengers travelling in open-sided carriages, the price was about 6d. With the extension complete, the original terminus of the PLR at Deepdale Street closed to passengers and became a goods depot, serving a growing population and innumerable mills during Preston's Industrial Revolution.

Preston's industrial base at the Deepdale Sidings was dominated by several industries. Horrocks Crewdson had their own No. 1 and 2 roads, to service the mills with fuel and carry-out their trade in textile manufacture. The sidings also incorporated Thomas Banks (coal merchants) and several coal trains a day brought in industrial and domestic coal from Lancashire pits, for redistribution from Deepdale.

On 14 January 1850, the railway infrastructure at Maudland became even more complex, when the PWR was linked to the FP&WRJR A second crossing was installed a short distance north of the original crossing to the first Maudland Station, for goods trains working through from Preston, which now had to reverse along the PWR and cross the Lancaster to Preston line on the level to reach a new extension linking Maudland with the Longridge line. This unwieldy operation necessitated two crossing keepers being on duty to prevent accidents at the two crossings on the level of the Lancaster & Carlisle Railway, one keeper looking after the PWR and the other supervising the FP&WRR crossing.

Deepdale Bridge Station opened on the same date as Maudland Bridge Station and was situated to the east of Maudland Tunnel, adjacent to the bridge carrying Deepdale Road. The station building was built on two levels, with an up and down platform reached by steps and a footbridge with waiting rooms on both platforms. Significantly, the main building was the administrative headquarters of the FP&WRR By 1867, this station had been renamed plain Deepdale. It was ideally situated to serve those attending the newly established Preston North End football ground, which was to become the home of the renowned 'Preston Invincibles.' Indeed, to cope with increased passenger numbers, the LNWR was to extend the station platform from ninety to one hundred yards.

Hewitson alluded to the characteristics of the two new stations in disparaging terms: 'In connection with the Longridge line, there are two stations at Preston one in Deepdale Road, the other in Maudland Road and both are of a very paltry character, especially the latter, (Maudland Bridge Station) which consists of nothing more than a narrow platform and a wooden sentry-like box, from which the tickets are issued.' [41]

In 1854, an intermediate station had been opened at Gamull Lane, Ribbleton, this being a two-storey detached building with distinctive architecture incorporating the usual facilities, and probably housed successive stationmasters. Access to the single platform was reached by a ramp from Gamull Lane and, although the station still stands, there is unfortunately no longer any trace of the original stone sleepers which formerly made up the platform edge. Curiously, the station was originally named Gammer Lane in timetables and certain railway documents. The station was renamed Fulwood from 1856, when a bridge was built to carry Gamull Lane over the railway.

The site of Maudland Bridge Station was alongside Maudland Road and located on a bridge over the Preston to Kendal Canal; the original bridge parapet is shown here next to Maudland Curve Signal Box. This was erected in 1886 to control the sidings and the junction of the Longridge line with the connection to Preston Station. Courtesy: G. Coltas

Deepdale Bridge Station looking towards the Maudland Tunnel, illustrating the station footbridge which linked the two platforms. Courtesy: George Whiteman Collection

Deepdale Bridge Station was opened by the Fleetwood Preston and West Junction Railway and originally housed the company offices. It is shown here in June 1953, complete with original features and still largely intact. Courtesy: Gordon Biddle

The entrance to Deepdale Bridge Station in June 1953. Twenty-three years after closure, it was appropriately named 'Station Fruit Shop'. The engraved word 'station' is shown above the original entrance to the lower level station buildings, which have since been demolished. Courtesy: Gordon Biddle

Ribbleton Station was situated adjacent to Gamull Lane Bridge and is shown here as a private house in 1952. The station first opened in 1854, and was originally named Gamull Lane, pronounced Gammer Lane. Ribbleton Station was the scene of the worst train crash on the line, occurring in August 1867. Courtesy: Gordon Biddle

The single stone platform at Ribbleton Halt, *c.* 1952, which was open for only a few years from 1863 and was accessed from Hamilton Road/Stuart Road. The halt saw occasional use by troops, from the nearby Fulwood Barracks, but, by 1952, the armies of yesteryear had long since faded into history. Courtesy: George Whiteman Collection

South of Fulwood Station, near to Cromwell Road, a small halt, also bearing the name Ribbleton, existed between 1863 and 1 June 1868 and saw occasional use by troops from the nearby Fulwood Barracks. [42] Following closure of this halt in 1868, the nearby station of Fulwood was more accurately named Ribbleton from 1 October 1900. Significantly, the May 1866 timetable featured four weekday trains to Longridge, calling at all four intermediate stations which, at that time, were Deepdale Bridge, Ribbleton, Fulwood and Grimsargh. The trains stopped at the platform outside the Plough Inn, Grimsargh, where facilities inside the pub included a booking office. In 1849, the FP&WRR Company owned the newly-built Station Hotel (Towneley Arms) at Longridge and before Longridge Station opened in 1872, tickets for trains were issued here. In 1851, the hotel became known as the Towneley Arms, but, owing to the precarious financial state of the company at that time, was disposed of during the same year. The original stations at Grimsargh and Longridge remained in use until new stations were built in 1870 and 1872 respectively.

By the late 1850s, passengers exploring Ribblesdale were able to book from Maudland Bridge to destinations not served directly by the railway, including Chipping, Ribchester and Stonyhurst, with carriages timed to meet the trains at Longridge. Those passengers about to enjoy a walk in 1859, however, complained about the constraints of Sunday trading, observance of the Sabbath and excessive drinking by others curtailing their own activities: 'We reached our journey's end at the Towneley Arms, which prepared us for the stroll higher up in the country. We cannot stay much longer, for here the foolishness of the enactment as to Sunday trading has made itself felt; we know we are travellers, but the moment the bell tolls for church we must be away. Because a number of fellows all over the country have disgraced themselves by getting drunk on Sunday, all of the rest of mankind must be treated as drunkards too.' [43]

The *Preston Pilot* reported that the leisure pursuits of children were catered for, when over 1,500 young passengers from the parish church and All Saints Sunday School, Preston, invaded Longridge in August 1858. The party was conveyed in three separate excursion trains and, upon arrival at Longridge, the scholars enjoyed bands of music and explored the village and surrounds, before returning home the same evening.

All classes of society used the branch during the halcyon days of the mid-nineteenth century. Those of a more genteel and sedentary nature evidently relied upon the service, including the local squire, Colonel William Assheton Cross, of Red Scar Mansion, Grimsargh-with-Brockholes. In September 1864, he wrote a letter to his daughter, Katherine Ellen Cross, requiring the services of his groom and footman, Hodgson, to meet the local train: 'Everton, Thursday. My dear Kitty, I write a line to say that I come home tomorrow. Tell Hodgson to meet the 2.20 train, and as I have some luggage he had better bring the carriage.'

The distinctive horse-drawn carriage was of a type that would have been used by three generations of the Cross family residing at Red Scar during the nineteenth century. The sound of 'clip-clop', moving along the rough road surface, no doubt harmonised with the vibrant whistles and steam emissions of the engine at either of the local stations serving Red Scar, which would have been either Gammer Lane (latterly Ribbleton) or Grimsargh. In consideration of the identity of the locomotive type waiting at the head of the 2.20 p.m. train in 1864, it is known that there were signs of improvement in 1856, with the acquisition of a new pioneering steam locomotive.

Messrs. Beyer Peacock of Manchester built a brand new 0-4-2 coke-burning saddle-tank locomotive, named 'Gardner' and costing £1,600, to work with the original 'Addison'. It is worth recalling that 'Addison' first made its debut in 1848, when it inaugurated steam and was finally sold between 1856-1860, along with the two Bury 2-2-0s that were acquired in 1849. On 24 December 1860, a second new engine was obtained from Sharp Stewart & Co. This locomotive, like its predecessor, exhibited the name 'Addison' and was a coke burning 0-4-2. Thus, the engine at the head of the 2.20 p.m. train in 1864 would have been either 'Gardner' or 'Addison'.

The core of the company's stock on 30 June 1860 comprised 2 locomotives, 3 composite carriages – first and second; 16 third-class carriages; 51 stone wagons – large size; 50 stone wagons – small size; and 8 other wagons. [44] Technical details of the two locomotives are given in the table. [45]

Red Scar House at Grimsargh with Brockholes was home to three generations of the Cross family, most of whom used the branch throughout the Victorian era. Courtesy: Tom Heginbotham Collection

The name 'Gardner' was displayed on the casing of the saddle tank locomotive built in 1856. Courtesy: George Whiteman Collection

Drawing of 'Addison'; the second locomotive to bear the name was built in 1860. Author's Collection

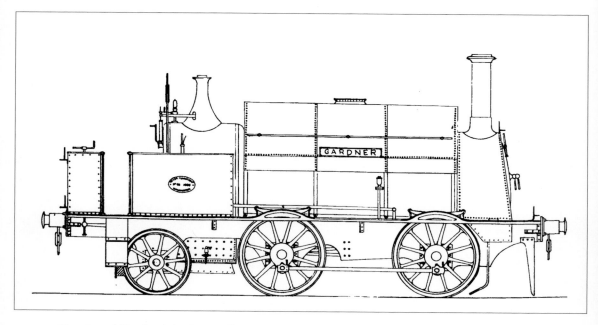

Drawing of 'Gardner'. Author's collection

	'Addison'	'Gardner'
Works No	1233	42
Subsequent classification	C5 Class L&YR	Undefined class
Inside cylinders	16in x 24in	14in x 20in
Coupled Wheels	5ft 0in	4ft 0in
Trailing Wheels	3ft 1in	3ft 0in
Wheelbase	7ft 2in + 6ft 8in	Not known
Boiler	3ft 8in x 10ft 2in	-do-
Pressure	120 lbs./in.	-do-
Heating Surface	873 sq. feet	692.8 sq. feet
Water	Not known	570 galls.
Weight	24tons 7cwt	22tons 6 cwt.

Renewed Railway Mania followed by Joint Ownership in 1866

By 1866, the fortunes of the reconstituted FP&WRR Company were such that management again foresaw the benefits of extending their line into West Yorkshire and consequently revived their plans. The parliamentary process was again invoked for the Company to build a railway via Hurst Green to Clitheroe and onto the Midland Railway at Elslack. A Bill reached committee stage, but there was opposition from the Lancashire & Yorkshire and the London & North Western Railways who, with the exception of the independent Longridge line, held the monopoly of Lancashire's railway lines.

These giant companies foresaw that their competitor, the Midland Railway Company, would have easy access to Preston via the PLR and therefore the proposals of the independent FP&WRR Company were perceived as a threat. In order to avert this, negotiations took place with the FP&WRR, culminating in an extraordinary General Meeting that was held by the directors of the FP&WRR on 5 June 1866, at 9 Winckley Street, Preston: 'The meeting was for the purpose of considering and approving an agreement of 12 May 1866, for the sake of the company's entire undertaking to the London & North Western and Lancashire & Yorkshire Railway Companies, upon certain terms to be stated'. Signed T. B. Addison (Chairman) and B. Walmsley (Secretary.) [46]

An agreement was effected on 1 July 1866, to transfer the PLR to the joint ownership of the London & North Western and Lancashire & Yorkshire Railway Companies (LNWR & L&YR). Statutory procedures were thus invoked to consign yet another company born of railway mania, the FP&WRR, to the annals of history. Compared with what might have been, the white elephant of Ribblesdale as symbolised by the remote railway cutting near Hurst Green is today the haunt of only curious historians and flocks of sheep.

CHAPTER FOUR

Combined LNWR and L&YR Ownership

This chapter covers the PLR while under the combined LNWR and L&YR joint ownership between 1867 and the end of the Victorian era. The principal legislation governing the takeover by the Joint Company was the FP&WRR Vesting Act, dated 17 June 1867, and jointly vested in the LNWR and L&YR Companies. In accordance with Section 11 of the Act, the FP&WRR was to be dissolved. Under Section 14, the affairs of the Company were to be managed by a joint committee of five directors from each company, which was to be known as the Preston & Longridge Joint Committee and which met in Liverpool once a month. This first committee underwent a change of management in 1889, when under Section 68 of the LNWR Act of 7 August 1888, the Preston and Longridge Joint Committee of 1867 was merged into the LNWR and L&YR Joint Committee as from 1 January 1889. [47]

The L&YR railway absorbed all the locomotives and rolling stock, while the LNWR assumed responsibility for the operation and maintenance of the line. The consortium purchased the steam locomotives, 'Addison' and 'Gardner', on 17 June 1867 from the former company, for immediate use. Both locomotives were modified to burn coal instead of coke between 1868 and 1872, and were subsequently withdrawn in 1874 and sent to Miles Platting, the locomotive works of the L&YR. [48] 'Gardner' was converted to a 0-4-0 tender-engine and, together with 'Addison', was sent to Scotland for use on the Wigtownshire Railway but, due to instability, 'Gardner' was then rebuilt in 1882 as a 0-4-0 saddle-tank. The pair were withdrawn and scrapped in 1894. [49]

Contemporary passenger and goods locomotives working through to Longridge comprised the various classes of the LNWR, while it was usual for L&YR locomotives and stock from the coalmines to work through to Deepdale Junction, before reversing into Deepdale yard. Following the withdrawal of 'Addison' and 'Gardner', the LNWR introduced John Ramsbottom's DX Class 0-6-0s (constructed in September 1858) onto the branch. A total of 943 of these engines were subsequently built for the L&YR and LNWR and the numbers

A relic of the joint ownership is shown on the wicket gate at the side of Grimsargh level crossing. This LNWR/L&YR Joint Lines notice warns persons to shut and fasten the gate; failure to do so invoked a penalty of forty shillings. Courtesy: HCC/RMC

remain the highest for any class of railway engine ever built in this country. [50]

Following construction at Crewe works between 1880 and 1883, Webb 'Cauliflower' Class 0-6-0 goods engines began to appear alongside the DX locomotives and became the mainstay of freight work during the 1920s. The luxury of enclosed coaches came when the LNWR introduced new stock in 1867 and which duly served an influx of workers, who travelled by train to work in the quarrying and textile industries. Before the days of electric lights, a railwayman with a torch ran along the tops of the non-corridor coaching stock that worked the branch, lifting lids and igniting the gas-jets below. Management could also look forward to attracting greater social and commercial interest from local businessmen, particularly if the anticipated link with Preston Station was constructed. The march of progress was exemplified with the acquisition of new carriages, which meant that 3rd class passengers could now dispense with their umbrellas in the previously open carriages. The *Preston Chronicle* of 27 June 1868, referred to some of the foregoing issues: 'A few months ago those who were under the unfortunate necessity of going in a 3rd class carriage to that place (Longridge) in wet weather had to keep their umbrellas up as well inside the train as out. This state of things has now been remedied. The present company have provided for ordinary traffic a very commodious train of three carriages coupled with a patent brake, which for the heavy incline will be of great service. What is now wanted to make the improvements complete is that the trains

LONDON AND NORTH WESTERN RAILWAY.

NORTHERN DIVISION.

PRESTON DISTRICT.

SHUNTING ENGINE
AND
LOCAL TRIP
WORKING BOOK.

MAY, 1920, and until further advised.

The timing and working of Trips and Shunting Engines in the PRESTON AREA will be as detailed, and each Shunting and Trip Engine must carry a target, corresponding with the number shown in this Book.

The Trips must not be held for any connection, and if the traffic is not ready, they must be sent away without it, unless authority to keep the Train is first obtained from the Preston Control Office.

The finishing time as shewn in bold print directly under the Trip etc., number represents the time at which the Engine must be released by the Traffic Department and sent to the Shed, and all concerned must see that the Engines are released promptly at the times laid down.

Arrangements must be made for Enginemen and Shunters working with Shunting Engines, where the working is continuous, to have an interval of 20 minutes for Meals between the 3rd and 5th hours of duty, at the most convenient opportunity.

As far as possible the Control Office must arrange by 4.0 p.m. daily for all special power required during the following day, and the Locomotive Foreman at each Shed as well as the Goods Guards Clerk, must be advised at that time of the requirements.

S. B. CARTER,

LIME STREET STATION, LIVERPOOL,   District Superintendent.
April, 1920.

No. 21.
"D.X." Engine.

7.35 a.m. to 5.30 p.m., Saturdays excepted.
7.35 a.m. to 3.30 p.m., Saturdays only.

	arr. (MO) dep.		arr. (MS) dep.		arr. (SO) dep.	
	a.m.	a.m.	a.m.	a.m.	a.m.	a.m.
Preston Loco. Shed	...	7 35	...	7 35	...	...
Maudlands	7 50	8 15	7 50	8 15	7 50	8 15
Grimsargh	8 30	8 40	8 30	8 40	8 30	8 40
Longridge	8 50	10 20	8 50	10 20	8 50	9 37
Grimsargh	10 25	10 40	10 25	10 40	...	...
Maudlands	10 50	11 35	10 50	11 15	9 57	10 20
				p.m.		
Deepdale	11 45	11 50	11 25	12 20E.&	...	...
		p.m.				
Maudlands	...	...	12 30	1 5	...	...
Grimsargh	...	...	...	...	...	...
Deepdale	...	...	1 15	1 25	...	...
	p.m.	p.m.				p.m.
Longridge	12 10	4 15	1 45	4 15	10 50	12 45
					p.m.	
Grimsargh	4 20	4 25	4 20	4 25	...	...
Deepdale	...	...	...	...	1 5	*2 40
Maudlands	4 35	4 50	4 35	4 50	2 45	2 55
Preston (N.U. Yard)	5 0	...	5 0	...	3 0	...

* Engine runs light to Loco. Shed at 1.25 p.m., and train is worked forward by No. 13 trip engine.

On Mondays relievers to travel passenger by 1.45 p.m. train, and effect relief at Longridge.

No. 22.
"D.X." Engine.
12.10 a.m. to 6.45 a.m., Mondays excepted.

	arr. (M)	dep.
	a.m.	a.m.
Preston Loco. Shed	...	12 10
„ Ribble Sidings	12 20	12 30
„ N.U. Yard	12 35	12 50
Greenbank	12 55	1 15
Oxheys	1 20	1 50
Greenbank	1 55	2 20
Preston N.U. Yard	2 25	3 0
Loco. Shed	3 5	3 30
Preston N.U. Yard	3 35	3 50
Farington	4 0	4 30 E. & B.
Leyland	4 35	5 10
Farington	5 15	6 10
Maudlands	6 25	...

To work Loco. coal empties off Shed to Farington at 3.30 a.m., and Leyland wagons to Farington at 5.10 a.m.

Preston Trip Working—**B**

Extract from the shunting engine and local trip working book, showing a DX engine working the PLR in May 1920. Courtesy: Mike Atherton Collection

No. 13.

"D.X." Engine.

5.55 a.m. to 3.40 p.m., Mondays and Saturdays excepted.

5.55 a.m. to 4.10 p.m., Mondays only.

5.55 a.m. to 12.55 p.m., Saturdays only.

	arr.	dep.
	a.m.	a.m.
Preston Loco. Shed	...	5 55
Maudlands	6 10	6 20
Deepdale	6 35	11 20 (marshalled as a Garswood train and forward with fresh engine from Maudlands).
		p.m.
Maudlands	11 25	12 30
	p.m.	
Deepdale	12 40	3 40 (On M O runs to Maudlands, due 3.50 p.m. On MS works 3.40 p.m. to Sanderson's Sdgs. On SO works forward from Deepdale 12.45 p.m. from Longridge to Preston. See No. 21 Trip).

should run through to the Fishergate station. This would no doubt tend greatly to induce visitors to take up their temporary abode during the summer in the salubrious neighbourhood of Longridge, but the inconvenience to businessmen of having to walk through the town at the risk of missing the train debars many from entertaining such a project and it is therefore hoped that as we understand plans have been prepared for that object, they may be put into execution'.

Sadly, the railway started badly under the new management, when the most serious accident in the line's history occurred at Fulwood Station on 10 August 1867. The popularity of the Longridge Guild event saw two full passenger trains returning from Longridge to Preston. An excursion train departed from Longridge for Preston at 8.25 p.m. with a total of thirteen carriages and a brake and stopped at Grimsargh and Fulwood Stations for ticket examination. Such was the popularity of the Guild festivities that this train preceded a service train, departing from Longridge at 8.40 p.m., with a total of seventeen carriages and a brake. Due to a signalling error and a tail-light not being fitted to the rear of the excursion train, the service train collided with the rear of the former at Fulwood Station while that train was stationary alongside the platform for the guard to carry out his ticket inspection. [51] There was no loss of life, but about seventy-five passengers, most of whom had Preston addresses, sustained mainly head and eye injuries. The locomotive 'Addison' survived comparatively well, with damage amounting to £20.

An abridged newspaper report described the scene of the accident: 'A very violent collision occurred, the catastrophe was instantaneous, and the alarm was tremendous. The actual injury sustained through the accident also intensified the seriousness of affairs as well as the time at which the disaster happened, along with the fact that some, if not all, of the carriages, were without lights. The scene was indescribable. Smashed carriages, people pitched about in them in all directions, bleeding faces, broken hats, moaning, screaming shouting on the rear carriages of the first train that was nearly crushed to pieces, and another had the top either partially or entirely broken off … Directly after the accident the engine of the front train was driven onto Preston for medical aid, and Dr. Marshall was, we understand, at the scene of the disaster in a short time'. [52]

Smith recalled the accident in his *A History of Longridge* (1888): 'Over sixty people were injured, several seriously. Strange to say no news of the accident reached Longridge until the following morning. Many hundreds of the visitors remained in the vicinity of the station waiting for the return of the train; and numbers had to sleep out of doors amid scenes of indescribable confusion'. [53]

Colonel W. Yolland carried out the official investigation into the cause of the accident and extracts from his report to the Board of Trade contain a number of interesting facts concerning operational working as well as the causation of the accident that are worthy of inclusion and are detailed in Appendix V.

During October 1870, a separate accident occurred at a crossing 500 yards from Longridge Station, when the engine, two carriages and the brake van derailed on the 5.40 p.m. Preston-bound train. Passengers sustained minimal injury and lost no time in alighting. The cause of the accident was thought to have been due to the mischievous meddling with a pair of points by a number of children who had been playing at the siding serving Chapel Hill quarry. The locomotive and tender were badly damaged and men successfully worked throughout the night to get it back onto the rails.

Features and Operational Considerations of the Established PLR

Precise details of all bridges and the major components of the signalling systems, together with operating details of each location, are further detailed in Appendix VII and VIII respectively. The plans (below) illustrate how the PLR and adjacent goods sidings served a diverse range of industries.

By far the most substantial structure on the PLR was the three-sectioned 862 yards long Maudland Tunnel (Bridges 7, 8, 9). There were originally twenty-two culverts, bridges and tunnels, numbered sequentially between Maudland Bridge and Longridge. Well-known over-bridges included those at Cromwell Road (Bridge 13), Gamull Lane (Bridge 15) and the extant bridge at Preston Road, Grimsargh (Bridge 17). At Grimsargh and in accordance with a local road safety committee's recommendations, a footbridge for school children attending St Michael's School was built alongside Bridge 17 in 1944. The last structure of the line, Bridge 22, was the tunnel leading to Longridge quarries, which remains to this day as testament to the town's quarrying industry.

During the twentieth century, new footbridges were installed at Porter Street, Deepdale (12A) alongside the narrow Gamull Lane Bridge (14A) and between Sulby Drive and St Maria Goretti's School at Ribbleton (15A). A distinctive road bridge carrying Deepdale Mill Street (12B) was erected in 1914. [54] The march of progress decreed that the last major bridge to be built on the line was numbered 15B and it carried the line over the original Preston bypass. The M6 motorway was opened by the Prime Minster, Harold Macmillan, in 1957 and had the distinction of being the first motorway in the country.

During November 1870, the Postmaster at Preston granted permission for telegraph poles to be placed along the line and a telegraph control system was introduced in 1872. [55] During 1877, the Joint LNWR/L&YR published their by-laws, rules and regulations concerning the PLR, which provide further insight into day-to-day workings. There were two sets of indicated 'catch or switch points' situated either side of Longridge Station, designed to curtail the actions of runaway trains by throwing them off the rails on the steeply graded line: 'Drivers and guards must be careful, should their train come to a standstill upon the catch points and they have an occasion to set back, or in working of single-line in case of obstruction, to see that the points are held over by some competent person'.

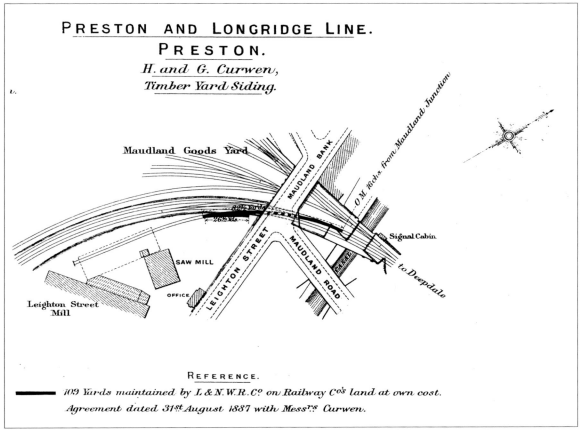

The commencement of the PLR at Maudland illustrating the complexity of goods sidings and the point where the PLR crossed over the Preston to Kendal canal and passed Maudland Curve Signal Box. Courtesy: Mike Atherton

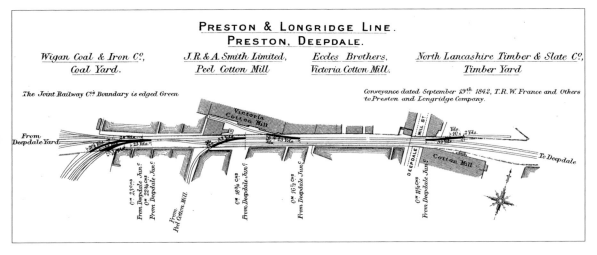

A section of the original PLR showing the main goods sidings at Deepdale, and the industries served by the railway. Courtesy: Mike Atherton

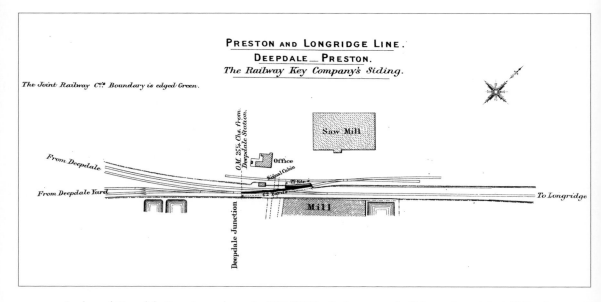

A plan of Deepdale Junction, where the FP&WRR of 1850 veered-off from the original PLR of 1840. Courtesy: Mike Atherton

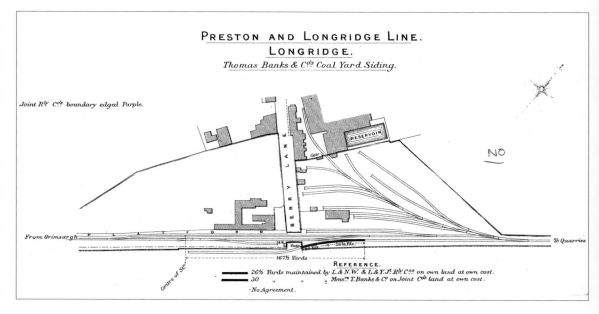

Coal yard sidings were situated east of Berry Lane level crossing where there was provision for livestock and general freight traffic. Beyond the goods yard an extension led to Messrs Hayhurst and Marsden's Cramp Oak Mill next to the reservoir. Longridge & District Local History Society

Above: On a gradient of 1 in 105 the line passed under an unusual brick footbridge, linking Porter Street with Castleton Road, constructed at Deepdale in 1914. Courtesy: Ian Race

Right: These catch points were situated between Longridge Station and Stone Bridge. George Whiteman Collection

Below: The eastern portal to Maudland Tunnel. David Hindle Collection

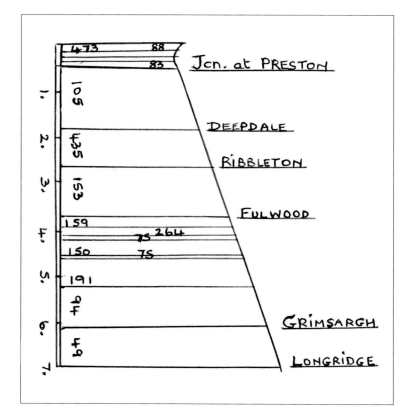

Gradient Profile of the PLR, clearly indicating that the steepest gradients on the branch were between Grimsargh and the Longridge quarries. Courtesy: Christine Dodding

Catch points were also used on the PLR at junctions with goods yards and sidings, to prevent unauthorised, uncontrolled or accidental access to the main line and, therefore, it was common for them to operate in tandem with the points controlling entry to the sidings.

Steep gradients, especially on the approach to Longridge, meant that it was important for hard-working engine crews to be fully co-ordinated, while knowing the topography of the branch: 'Attention is especially called to the following inclines, where particular care is required: From Maudland to Ribbleton raising for one and three quarter miles on a gradient of 1 in 106; from Fulwood to Grimsargh, raising for two miles on a gradient of 1 in 150; from Grimsargh station towards Longridge raising for half a mile on a gradient of 1 in 191; from five to 6 mile post raising for one a half miles on a gradient of 1 in 94; and from 6 mile post to Longridge raising on a gradient of 1 in 50'.

The standardised signalling system of the LNWR was adopted in 1882. Signals along the line were initially LNWR lower-quadrant, some of which lasted well into the 1960s. New signal boxes were incorporated at Maudland Curve, Deepdale Junction, and Longridge by 1885. As there were signals, points and crossings remote from the actual signal boxes, a number of 'Annett's keys' were used. These were kept in a 'lock' in the signal-cabin lever-frames and taken to a specified location by the train crew. The key would then be placed in point levers, crossing gates or ground frames, to enable shunting or traffic movement. [56]

After January 1929, the LMS began to install a new type of signal, with a yellow arm and a black chevron displaying an amber light at night to help distinguish them from stop signals. These distant signals provided drivers with an advance warning of the stop signals ahead; they could be passed in the horizontal or 'on' position. On the Longridge branch, all distant signals were fixed in the 'on' position, which was common practice at complex junctions and branch lines where line speeds were low. British Railways upper-quadrant (where the signal was raised 45 degrees from the horizontal) replaced some signals along the line in later years. The four main level crossings were situated at Deepdale Mill Street, Skeffington Road, Long Sight Lane, Grimsargh and Berry Lane, Longridge. The single-track section was without any crossing loops at the intermediate stations of Ribbleton and Grimsargh and therefore operated with strict adherence to a system of 'one-engine-in-steam'. Originally, the double section of track between Maudland and Deepdale Junction was worked as two separate single-lines, with a train staff system. The south line identified as being next to the main platforms at Maudland and at Deepdale Bridge was to be used by passenger trains on the one-engine-in-steam principle, while the north line was for the use of goods trains. [57]

A close-up of the staff that authorised trains to pass between Deepdale Junction and Longridge. This was the driver's authority to enter the single-line section and confirmed that his train was the only one in the section. The name of the section of line to which the staff applied was cast into the metal portion. Courtesy: Alan Castle

Deepdale Junction on 19 October 1978. Class 40 No. 40180 is bound for Courtaulds and class 47 No. 47215 is shown reversing up to Deepdale coal sidings. After Skeffington Road level crossing, the line towards Longridge merged into a single track. Courtesy: Alan Summerfield

Class 40 No. 40.339 is given the road to Deepdale Sidings by the original LNWR signals at Deepdale Junction on 10 May 1972. Courtesy: Peter Fitton

Stanier Class 8F 2-8-0 No. 48438, on freight to Longridge, passes Deepdale Junction Signal Box on 4 July 1966. A well practiced exchange of the staff from signalman to the driver meant that the driver had to be in possession of the staff before he entered the single-line section. Courtesy: Peter Fitton

Stanier 2-8-0 No. 48679 passes the distant signal at Greenland's Estate, Ribbleton. Courtesy: Alan Castle

Above: Class 25 No. 25.321, from Warrington Arpley yard, propels its load of coal hoppers across the level crossing at Deepdale Mill Street, on 3 May 1985, to reach the coal distribution centre. Courtesy: Martin Hilbert

Left: Stanier 8F 2-8-0 No. 48438 at Grimsargh Goods Yard on 4 July 1966. Courtesy: Peter Fitton

A view of the goods yards and the Towneley Arms/station, Longridge, looking towards Preston.
Courtesy: George Whiteman Collection

New Stations for Grimsargh and Longridge

The improvisation of the Plough Inn as a station building at Grimsargh, at a rent of £204.3.11*d* per annum, came to an end in 1870, when a board meeting of the Joint Committee concluded that an entirely new station was needed: 'Owing to the many means of egress from the platform at Grimsargh station, great difficulties arose in the proper collection of tickets; the companies paid an annual rent of £6 to the adjoining public house for the use of one of the rooms as a booking office, through which a door led into the house. It was recommended that a small piece of land be purchased from a Dr. Goss and that an independent station be built thereon at a cost say of £200'. [58]

The new station was a single-storey structure built of Longridge stone and was situated almost opposite the Plough Inn, on the south side of Long Sight Lane, adjacent to the level crossing. It was typical of the genre of L&YR branch line stations, although there was never a station canopy. It provided improved facilities for passengers, parcels and livestock, along with a cattle-loading dock that was located at the western end of the single platform. Goods and coal sidings were situated behind the station. The Plough Inn was now able to offer more accommodation to customers. The old slotted shelf that used to hold railway tickets, is, to this day, concealed by plaster.

Grimsargh Station was built in 1870 and is pictured here in LMS days before closure of the passenger service in 1930, with gas lamps and the station name of Grimsargh still in place. Courtesy: Tom Heginbotham Collection

Longridge Station with the incorporated Towneley Arms Public House built onto the station buildings. The rather curious mini-signal box features in this view looking towards the quarry extension. Courtesy: Alan Summerfield Collection

WD 'Austerity' Class 8F 2-8-0 No. 90675 stands alongside Longridge Signal Box. Courtesy: Alan Castle

Longridge level crossing showing signal box, goods yard and goods warehouse. Courtesy: Longridge & District Local History Society

WD 'Austerity' Class 8F 2-8-0 No. 90675 stands at the water tower opposite Longridge Station on 22 August 1964, just before commencing the return journey to Preston. Courtesy: Alan Castle

Viewed from Berry Lane level crossing, an unidentified Stanier locomotive pauses near to a primitive hand crane and warehouse in Longridge goods yard during 1966. Courtesy: Longridge & District Local History Society

The Longridge quarrying industry prospered during the 1870s, with up to four hundred men producing about 30,000 ton of stone per week. Many men arrived at Longridge by train and consequently, better station facilities were required for all sections of the community. In 1872, the Joint Committee repurchased the Towneley Arms at Longridge and land adjacent thereto for £2,900 and erected a new station with a canopy as an adjunct to the hotel. The *Preston Chronicle* reported: 'The purchase of the Towneley Arms will no doubt prove of great benefit to the public as well as to the railway authorities. A space will be afforded for larger and more convenient offices and waiting room, both of which have been somewhat deficient'. [59] On 25 February 1886, the Towneley Arms reverted to more traditional use as a public house when it was duly reported that 'station alterations at Longridge are nearly completed but on completion the hotel connection with the platform will be cut off, at an estimated cost of £80'. [60]

An Improving Service Benefiting the Community

Analysis of the history of the line during a period of economic sustainability, which was predominantly towards the end of the Victorian era and into the first two decades of the twentieth century, gives an insight into how the line served workers at both work and play. In turn this increased usage led to the establishment of a direct link between the detached Maudland Bridge Station and Preston Station in 1885.

Contemporary newspaper reports suggest that mill and quarry workers formed a significant proportion of the passengers carried throughout the heyday of the industrial revolution. The Factory Acts of 1847 and 1850 saw a reduction to a ten-and-a-half-hour day and the implementation of half-day working on Saturday, while the Sabbath was normally a day of rest. With more time to spare at weekends the public increasingly came to depend upon the passenger service for both work and leisure.

The passenger service embraced interspersed excursion trains during the annual wakes holiday period. Although there was never a direct regular passenger service linking the Fleetwood line to the PLR, an excursion train from Kirkham ran through to Longridge in July 1868: 'On Wednesday there was a cheap trip to Longridge and back from Kirkham. At Maudland the carriages were detached and ran on to the Longridge line to convey the excursionists. The excursionists, on arriving, scattered themselves among the hills and many were expressions of gratification at the romantic scenery and the natural beauties of the place. The return train left Longridge at 5.40pm, to be joined to the 6.35pm, train to Kirkham. Such an excursion perhaps never before visited Longridge'. [61]

On 3 July 1872, passengers, including those from outlying villages close to the line, were encouraged to enjoy the thrills of the big top in Preston, doubtless attracted by an advertisement in the *Preston Guardian*: 'Newsome's Grand

Circus – adjoining the railway station, Butler Street, Preston, immense success of last night's Cinderella – notice to the inhabitants of Longridge, Goosnargh, Fulwood and neighbourhood, a special train will leave Preston tomorrow, Thursday evening at a quarter to eleven, for the accommodation of parties from that locality visiting the circus'.

The importance of the branch line was such that in 1883, the inhabitants of Longridge campaigned for an improved service with more trains each way on the branch: 'We, the undersigned, being inhabitants of Longridge and district, do herewith respectfully request you to ask the owners of the PLR to at once renew the 8pm train from Maudland, and the 8.30p.m train from Longridge; and also to alter the 6.30pm and the 7.15pm train from Maudland and Longridge respectively, to 8pm. and 8.30pm on Sundays, thus assimilating the train service. Our reasons for memorialising you are, that great and serious inconvenience and expense are caused to many residents in the district by reason of there being no later trains from Preston and Longridge than the 6.20pm and the 7.30pm respectively'.[62] Signed (a total of 139 names).

Extension of the Line from Maudland to Preston Station

The passenger service was increased and by 1884 up to eight weekday trains were diagrammed. A direct Maudland link with Preston Station was long overdue and, accordingly, tenders were opened for various works required for the widening of the railway bridge over the canal and the making of new bridges under Leighton Street and Maudland Road. A certain Mr McGregor's tender of £7,353 was subsequently accepted. [63] 'A reported inspection by the Board of Trade took place on 16th May 1885, prior to the intended opening of the line on 1st June 1885, the day before which the cross roads (PWR) will be taken out'. [64]

Coinciding with the installation of the link, the PWR junction was completely removed, the spartan Maudland Bridge Station was closed the same day and a new Maudland Curve Signal Box was opened. At the same time the complex railway infrastructure at Maudland changed dramatically and both crossings on the level of the LCR were removed during 1885.

The sharply-curved loop line provided the facility for Longridge trains to use the main platforms at Preston Station for the first time. It was undoubtedly more convenient, because passengers no longer had to walk, or to be conveyed, into the town centre, despite reported problems in relation to the new timetable. Shortly after the link was established, the *Preston Herald* carried a report on the level of dissatisfaction: 'The new train service which commenced on Monday last on the Preston to Longridge line is far from giving general satisfaction, especially to the working classes, who allege that under the revised timetable they lose more than they gain by the changes that have been made. Under the old arrangements a train started from Longridge at 1.45 p.m. This train was very convenient for those employed in mills and other workshops, more especially on Saturday afternoon, when a large number always travelled to Preston, some having business of importance which they were just in time to transact, while others went marketing. The earliest train by which the operatives can now leave Longridge on a Saturday afternoon is at 3.30 p.m., arriving at Preston at 4 p.m., by which time it will be dark during the greatest portion of the day ... The trains have been timed to meet others going out from the central station at Preston ... It cannot be denied that the working classes are entitled to a train that they can get into Preston at about 2 p.m., at least on Saturdays'. [65]

Author Tom Smith evidently felt compelled to put pen to paper, to highlight the plight of workmen who were concerned about arriving on time for their shift in Preston: 'Along with most people in the locality I quite appreciate the advantage that doubtless will in due course accrue to us through the connection of passenger trains with the central station at Preston. But these advantages will have been gained at too heavy a price if the service of trains which came into force on the first is to be a fixture ... Under the new service workmen cannot get to Preston at a convenient time and on a week night cannot get to Preston at all. Surely, in these days, even railway companies ought to pay attention to the convenience of the greater number. If not, a little practical competition may show them that they are quite omnipotent. In conclusion, I would observe that, while an afternoon train on Sunday is a most desirable innovation it would be the means of effecting far more good were it run at least an hour earlier. (Signed) Tom Smith, Longridge'. [66]

PRESTON & LONGRIDGE RAILWAY.

List of Passenger Fares from the undermentioned Stations:--

FROM	TO	SINGLE JOURNEY TICKETS			RETURN TICKETS		
		First Class.	Second Class.	Gov. Class.	First Class.	Second Class.	Gov. Class.
		s. d.	s. d.	s. d.	s. d.	s. d.	s. d.
PRESTON (Fishergate Station)	DEEPDALE ..	0 4	0 3	0 1½			
	FULWOOD ...	0 8	0 5	0 3			
	GRIMSARGH ..	0 11	0 7	0 5	1 6	1 0	0 8
	LONGRIDGE ..	1 3	0 11	0 7	2 0	1 6	1 0
DEEPDALE	PRESTON (Fishergate)	0 4	0 3	0 1½			
	FULWOOD ...	0 4	0 3	0 1½			
	GRIMSARGH ..	0 9	0 6	0 3½	1 3	0 10	0 6
	LONGRIDGE ..	1 0	0 9	0 5½	1 8	1 3	0 10
FULWOOD	PRESTON (Fishergate)	0 8	0 5	0 3			
	DEEPDALE ..	0 4	0 3	0 1½			
	GRIMSARGH ..	0 4	0 3	0 1½			
	LONGRIDGE ..	0 8	0 6	0 4			
GRIMSARGH	PRESTON (Fishergate)	0 11	0 7	0 5	1 6	1 0	0 8
	DEEPDALE ..	0 9	0 6	0 3½	1 3	0 10	0 6
	FULWOOD ...	0 4	0 3	0 1½			
	LONGRIDGE ..	0 6	0 4	0 2			
LONGRIDGE	PRESTON (Fishergate)	1 3	0 11	0 7	2 0	1 6	1 0
	DEEPDALE ..	1 0	0 9	0 5½	1 8	1 3	0 10
	FULWOOD ...	0 8	0 6	0 4			
	GRIMSARGH ..	0 6	0 4	0 2			

June 1st, 1885.

T. H. CARR, *Secretary*.

List of fares on the Preston to Longridge railway as at 1 June 1885. Courtesy: Mike Atherton Collection

Left: This ornate Lancashire and Yorkshire Railway timetable for 1888 featured the Preston to Longridge branch.

Below: Services on this timetable incorporated the Preston & Longridge timetable between 2 July and 30 September 1888 showing that trains stopped at the intermediate stations of Deepdale, Ribbleton, and Grimsargh (for Whittingham) and that the journey took twenty-five minutes.
Courtesy: Mike Atherton Collection

HORWICH BRANCH.

HORWICH TO CHORLEY, PRESTON, BLACKBURN, BOLTON, MANCHESTER, WIGAN, SOUTHPORT, AND LIVERPOOL.

(Detailed multi-column timetable of departures from Horwich, Blackrod, Chorley, Preston, Blackburn, Lostock Junction, Bolton, Manchester (No.8 Plat), Wigan, Southport, and Liverpool (Exchange) for Week Days and Sundays.)

LIVERPOOL, SOUTHPORT, WIGAN, MANCHESTER, BOLTON, BLACKBURN, PRESTON, AND CHORLEY TO HORWICH.

(Detailed multi-column timetable of departures from Liverpool (Exchange), Southport, Wigan, Manchester (No.6 Plat), Bolton, Lostock Junction, Blackburn, Preston, Chorley, Blackrod, and Horwich for Week Days and Sundays.)

* Departs from No. 5 Platform. † Arrives at No. 7 Platform. ‡ Passengers leave Manchester (No. 5 Platform) at 1-25 aft. from July 2nd to 13th inclusive.
§ Arrives at No. 6 Platform.   1st and 3rd class only to Manchester.

PRESTON TO LONGRIDGE AND BACK.

	WEEK DAYS.								SUNDAYS.					WEEK DAYS.								SUNDAYS.		
	1	2	3	4	5	6	7	8	1	2	3	4		1	2	3	4	5	6	7	8	1	2	3	4
				a													b								
	morn	morn	morn	aft	aft	aft	aft	aft	morn	aft	aft			morn	morn	noon	aft	aft	aft	aft	aft	morn	aft	aft
PRESTON (Fishergate) ...dep	6 45	9 0	11 20	12 45	2 0	4 50	6 10	7 55	9 37	2 55	7 15	...	LONGRIDGE ....dep	8 10	10 0	12 0	1 25	3 30	5 25	6 55	8 30	10 5	3 30	7 55
Deepdale .... "	6 51	9 6	11 26	12 50	2 6	4 56	6 16	8 1	9 43	3 1	7 21	...	Grimsargh	8 16	10 6	12 6	1 30	3 36	5 31	7 1	8 36	10 11	3 36	8 1
Fulwood .... "	6 56	9 11	11 31	...	2 11	5 1	6 21	8 6	9 48	3 6	7 26	...	Fulwood	8 21	10 11	12 11	...	3 41	5 36	7 6	8 41	10 16	3 41	8 6
Grimsargh .... "	7 3	9 18	11 38	12 59	2 18	5 8	6 28	8 13	9 55	3 13	7 33	...	Deepdale	8 27	10 18	12 18	1 40	3 48	5 42	7 13	8 48	10 23	3 48	8 13
LONGRIDGE ....arr	7 10	9 25	11 45	1 5	2 25	5 15	6 35	8 20	10 2	3 20	7 40	...	PRESTON (Fishergate) ...arr	8 33	10 25	12 25	1 45	3 55	5 48	7 20	8 55	10 30	3 55	8 20

a Saturdays only.   Starts from E. L. Island Platform.   b Saturdays only.

The passenger service was gradually improved and by 1888 the timetable maintained up to eight trains Monday to Saturday and three on Sunday. The reinstatement of a Saturday only train, departing from Longridge at 1.25 p.m. reaching Preston at 1.45 p.m., presumably addressed earlier concerns and was more socially acceptable. Interestingly the down 12.45 p.m. Saturday only train departing from Preston to Longridge was specifically shown to depart from the East Lancashire island platform and not the more usual Platform 2.

Overall, the provision of a direct link with Preston Station and the improved timetable began to encourage the use of the PLR by all sections of the community, including scholars attending the prestigious St John's College, a select preparatory school at Grimsargh: 'At the end of the mid summer-term 1891, after the closing service the boys packed their bags. On the following morning the students, numbering upwards of 100, left the Grimsargh station of the LNWR, shortly after 8 o'clock. Special carriages were provided by the railway company, and in due time the students all arrived safely at their various homes in England, Ireland, and Scotland'.

During 1898, the opportunity arose to a wide section of the travelling public to savour the atmosphere of showman George Green's travelling fair, which was being held at the Orchard in Preston. The fun of the fair would have invoked a marvellous cacophony of sound from the banging of drums, the music of steam-powered organs, shrieking whistles from traction engines and showmen vociferously vaunting their sideshows. There were menageries with daring lion-tamers, who loudly boasted of great acts of bravado and narrow escapes. Coconut shies and other forms of pleasure did a thriving business. Among the attractions were heavy weight lifters, dwarves, ghost illusionists, marionettes, and galleries, featuring the very first cinematographic performances in the town. Thus the first silent movies arrived in Preston in 1898, a popular media that was to provide additional passenger traffic for the railway. The public flocked to see the first black and white flickering films, heralding a blossoming industry with the emergence of up to twenty-two cinemas and five theatres/music halls in Preston alone, during the first half of the twentieth century.

CHAPTER FIVE

A Victorian Potpourri of Events

A scrupulously thorough search of primary sources has provided an illuminated, light hearted insight into the day-to-day running of the PLR as well as its Victorian heritage:

The Official Opening of the Preston to Longridge Line, May Day, 1840

'Yesterday, and a beautiful May day it was, for the opening of the railway from Preston to Longridge, a distance of something more than six miles. It had previously been intimated that conveyances would be prepared for Directors and friends. Second-class carriages were prepared, as the weather was favourable and some of the best horses, decorated with ribbons, from Mr Wilcockson's stud, he himself being the whip. A very comfortable number of persons were assembled in the carriages, as they moved at a good pace to the Plough Inn, Grimsargh. It had been arranged to stop there to watch a train of wagons, stone-laden, come down the steep incline and, afterwards, the Directors' carriages arrived at the terminus.

After remaining at Longridge an hour, while Mr Fleming's stupendous delph was visited, as well as the one belonging to the railway, the carriages moved off as if by magic, Mr Bushel, the engineer of the line acting as brakeman. He limited the speed to 8 m.p.h. to avoid accident and then to 20 m.p.h., half the speed it would have gone if the brake had been released. A mile from Preston, the speed decreased and the horses which had followed were attached and so they arrived at Preston without accident. Three hearty cheers were given. Many people had assembled on bridges and were astonished to see the carriages move without power. A party of Directors and friends dined at the Castle Inn and spent the evening most sociably drinking, Prosperity to the Longridge Railway.' [67]

The Arrival of the Iron Horse on Whit Monday, 1848

The *Preston Pilot* fittingly recorded the day's celebrations and carnival atmosphere that prevailed, when the indefatigable Chairman, Thomas Batty Addison, rode behind his namesake – the steam locomotive, from Deepdale Street to Longridge: 'Whit Monday was fixed for the fête, and about two hundred ladies and gentlemen (including a large party of officers of the 89th from Fulwood barracks) joined in its celebration. Eleven o'clock was the hour of assembly at the Deepdale Street station and shortly after that time the whole of the party were in attendance, and having taken their seats in the different carriages, the engine, was decorated with several Union Jacks, etc and a most handsome banner bearing the inscription "The Fleetwood Preston & West Riding Railway," was attached to the carriages, and the signal being given, the train was soon in motion, and going at a speed very different from that which had been attained on the old system. As most of our readers are aware, there is a steep incline for a very considerable portion of the distance (including some parts at one in forty five), so that the speed was occasionally relaxed.

'The admirable band of the 89th were in the first carriage, and played some lively airs while on the journey. The train having arrived at the Longridge terminus, the party formed in procession, and preceded by the band, marched through the village … A ramble was proposed and various parties were formed to climb the heights. Several parties went to peep at one of the immense reservoirs belonging to the Preston Waterworks Company, on which were majestically moving two large and beautiful swans.

'A large marquee had been erected for the luncheon … Thomas Batty Addison, Esq. (Chairman) and John Paley, Esq., occupied the head of each table. The refreshment provided was most ample and substantial, as indeed it had need to be, after a long stroll in the bracing and pure atmosphere of the Longridge fells. Speeches and toasts followed, and then the band signalled the dance. Various young ladies with their delighted partners tripped it lightly to the astonishment of villagers. Country dances and polkas followed and were heartily enjoyed by the ladies and their gallant partners. As all pleasure must come to an end, so had this delightful rural fete, and after regaining the road, the procession was again formed, and preceded by the band, retraced their steps through the village to the station, and having taken their seats in the carriages, were soon on the way to Preston, where they arrived without let or hindrance perfectly delighted with the treat which the Directors had so handsomely given them.' [68]

From Old Asthmatic Engines to Bovines and Boas (1849)

The carriage of passengers seems to have been of secondary importance, with at least one passenger witnessing bizarre happenings and an apparent lack of investment on the Longridge line, with first-class bovines and first-class passengers sharing the same compartment. A ceaseless watch for boa constrictors had to be maintained, as anything could happen in this wildlife habitat, although in later years the nearest I came to it was a colony of slow worms alongside the track. If this was an example of first-class travel, then what was travel like in third-class carriages during the late 1840s-50s?

'On Wednesday last I took it in my head to visit Longridge. I scrambled into a carriage, first-class of course, when to my surprise I found a quadruped in the shape of a fine calf, stretched within the compartment. Several other passengers noticed the same, but were given to understand that the practice was a common one, the Longridge Directors being no respecters of persons clean or unclean. Our journey, however, was not deficient in interest, for what with the wheezing puffs of the old asthmatic engine, the bleatings of the cow, and the imprecation of an old gentleman, whose juxtaposing with the calf appeared a grievous source of annoyance to him, we had music enough to spare. I had a deep veneration for the Longridge line, and therefore was extremely sorry to see so dirty and obnoxious a practice as that referred tolerated in the travelling arrangements. Would it be to too much to suggest that a separate box of some kind should be provided for the swine, etc. which are conveyed on this railway? If calves are to be located within a passenger carriage, why not cows; and if cows, why not bulls; and if bulls, why not the requisite accommodation for a rhinoceros or boa constrictor? The precedent is a dangerous one, and may grow into a great abuse'. [69]

A Double Fatal Accident Involving Man and Beast (1856)

At the Longridge end of the line, one of the first fatalities on the PLR occurred in July 1856, when a man and a horse were killed on an occupation crossing near Stone Bridge. 'At the subsequent inquest, the engine-driver said that, when he first whistled, the train was going between 20 and 30 miles an hour. He continued at that speed until he saw the horse, when he applied the brake, but, just as he did so, the train struck the horse. He had no steam on and, therefore, it would have been useless to reverse the engine. The driver did all that he could to prevent the collision and shouted to the deceased, who appeared to have heard him as he tried to pull back his horse. Verdict: Accidental Death'. [70]

Filthy Stories (1858)

Unfortunately the conduct of certain reprobate males in darkened carriages was to be found wanting towards the opposite sex. This was the age of Victorian respectability, and one newspaper correspondent using the pseudonym 'public decency,' felt compelled to provide evidence of falling standards on the

Longridge trains: 'Permit me, through your columns, to call the attention of the railway company to the necessity of placing lamps in their carriages, when the trains run in the evening. Last Sunday, a few persons entertained themselves, and their immediate friends, by the loud repetition of filthy stories to the annoyance of several parties at the further end of the carriage, amongst whom were several females. As the individuals were apparently in a respectable position in life, doubtless the exposure of their countenances to the gaze of the female strangers, who were compelled to listen to their filthy observations, would have modified to some extent their language. It is highly desirable that respectable persons, who may take their wives and children to inhale the fresh breezes on Longridge Fell, should be protected from such outrages.' [71]

'The Runaway Train came down the Line and she Blew ...' (1859)

The following describes a horrendous fatal accident, occurring in 1859 to a quarry worker, and how a more serious accident involving a runaway train was averted by the actions of a heroic boy and a station clerk at Grimsargh: 'A brakeman was on the front wagon, bringing three wagons heavily loaded with stone from the quarry towards Longridge. He attempted to apply the brake to test the velocity of the first wagon, but was unable to produce any effect upon the wheels, and in consequence he jumped to the wagon behind in order to use the brake. Whilst doing so he slipped down between the wagons, fell under the wheels, and was completely torn to pieces.

'As the wagons now had no check upon them, they dashed on past Longridge, and the declivity in the line gave them greater speed. When near Grimsargh, a boy observed them coming at a terrific speed, and he at once ran to the booking clerk at Grimsargh station. The clerk immediately went to a siding and changed the points. The wagons then came past the clerk at the rate of sixty miles per hour, ran on the siding and collided with some other wagons. After the crash, the first wagon was smashed to pieces, the second and third wagons were seriously damaged, and the stones they contained were thrown in all directions. Immediately after this had taken place, the usual passenger train from Preston, due at half past six, came up; and, had it not been for the presence of mind of the booking clerk, this train would undoubtedly have crashed and a large number of passengers would have been either killed or dreadfully injured'. [72]

Filthy Stations (1861)

In Victorian times, verbal and written attacks on the Longridge railway were commonplace. The directors were upbraided, the secretary lampooned, the carriages caricatured, the steam engine condemned, and the stations reviled by vandals. The secretary of the railway company, Mr Walmsley, replied to a complaining correspondent to the *Preston Chronicle* on 2 March 1861: 'We are now attacked by a gentleman who states that the stations are filthy and that there is a want of accommodation. I will grant to Mr. Catterall that, until the company build a new station at Grimsargh, there is a want of accommodation there; but there is ample for the traffic at other stations. The word filthy as applied to any of them is a gross exaggeration. On a wet and windy afternoon, a crowd of people will no doubt litter a room and soil a floor! The company have expended £1,352.11s.3d. within the last four years on the stations. The waiting rooms are furnished in a suitable way and they are cleaned daily. The company does not profess to give 1st-class accommodation. We have scarcely any 1st-class traffic, except a few season ticket holders who pay mere nominal rates. Mr. Catterall, for his whole family and two men servants, pays £10 per annum and, for this, he expects the arrangements of Euston and King's Cross.

'The second charge is that laden wagons are attached to passenger carriages going to Longridge. Mr. Catterall calls this a dangerous practice, but omits to say in what the danger consists. There is always, in addition to the guard in charge of the passenger carriages, a brakeman in charge of the last wagon, and if a wagon did get detached, it could be stopped instantly. Mr. Catterall should say what he is afraid of and I will endeavour to remove his fears. I can only say that no accident whatever has happened to a passenger train since the line was opened, except in one instance, when a man lost his life at Grimsargh, entirely through drunkenness'.

A Familiar Story of a Broken-down Train (1865)

To a certain extent history seems to have repeated itself with stories about frustrated passengers on broken down trains and people being late for work: 'The locomotive of the train leaving Preston at 7.15 am, broke down at Fulwood and a long delay ensued before it could proceed. This was a source of great disappointment to many parties, whose business required their presence in Preston at 9 o'clock and who could not come down to town by the usual morning train. Some of them came forward in a bus, whilst others walked to Preston'. [73]

So what's new? Today however it is not the sound of clickety-click, clickety-click of trains passing over rails, but a different era of modern lap tops and mobile phones with ring tones and warbles and the unavoidable eavesdropping on ultra-modern trains that raise a titter. 'Hi, I'm on the train, on the train, on the train. What's for tea? I attended a meeting this morning, it was ghastly! I seem to have been on the train all day, it must be tomorrow we are running late. Pick me up at 6 o'clock, no make it 7, can't wait to see you, pick me up at 7, sorry I mean 6, I think!'

Grimsargh level crossing gates showing the steep gradients beyond the signal on the road to Longridge and the joint LNWR/L&YR Station adjacent to the crossing (right). At the time Grimsargh (WHR) station site (left) was being redeveloped for housing. Courtesy: Tony Gillett

Grimsargh Level Crossing Gates reduced to Matchwood (1866)

At Grimsargh, there was no indicator to or from the signal box at Deepdale Junction and the porter normally operated the gates until 5.30 p.m. By October 1960, trainmen worked the gates and signals, the fireman opening the gates and the guard closing them, once the train had passed but, alas, due to unforeseen circumstances, this was not always the case. The gradient between Longridge and Grimsargh was a problem from the beginning and the level crossing bore the brunt of several accidents. Such an incident was reported in the *Preston Pilot* on 30 June 1866: 'A somewhat serious accident happened on the Longridge line. On making enquiries, it appears it was a simple affair. It seems that on Thursday morning the gate crossing the rails at Grimsargh was not opened in time for the stone train from Longridge and the wagons ran through it and, of course, smashed the woodwork to pieces. No-one was hurt and the damage will be covered by a trifle'.

A Chilling Accident at Deepdale Bridge Station (1866)

Unfortunately, things were not very festive at Deepdale Bridge Station during Christmas 1866. The station was the scene of a fatal accident involving Margaret Banks, a fifteen-year-old power loom weaver, who somehow managed to get her

Icy conditions and dereliction at the former Deepdale Bridge Station provide an atmospheric setting for a chilling Christmas ghost story. The station canopy on the Preston-bound platform played host to Margaret Banks and her friends in December 1866, when young Margaret was killed in a terrible accident. The girl in the crinoline dress is said to haunt the eerie blackness of the nearby Maudland Tunnel. Courtesy: Tony Gillett

Victorian crinoline entangled with a carriage door. Sadly, she was killed when she ended up under the wheels of a Preston-bound train. An inquest into the cause of death was held at Preston Coroner's Court, followed by the institution of criminal proceedings. In legal parlance the circumstances of the case are set out below:

'On the arrival at Deepdale station of the 2pm train from Longridge, Henry Whittaker, a wool-stapler of Haslingden, held his hand out of the carriage window to a group of girls who thought that he wished to pass something. Mary Flynn got to him first, but Margaret Banks pushed her to one side and said, "No let me have it". Whether Banks got hold of Whittaker's hand, or he seized hers, is not ascertained. When the train started to move, Banks walked on by the side of the track but, after a few yards, screamed out, fell, and was run over by the carriages and instantly killed. Some of the girls who had been with the deceased on the platform said that Whittaker held her hand, that he would not let her go, and that she screamed before she dropped between the platform and the carriages and was killed. After the accident Whittaker was arrested and bailed to appear at the Preston Inquest.

Mr Banks, the father of the deceased, was also present along with Mr. B. Walmsley, Secretary of the P.L.R. Company and several witnesses. Mary Ann Rush said that the girls had agreed to go to Maudland, but Whittaker took hold of the girl's hand and, when he had done so, the train gave a jerk. The train set off when he got hold of her hand and the witness (Rush) pulled the deceased and said, "Maggie, Maggie, leave loose", but she could not. The witness saw her going by the side of the train and her clothes getting fast, so she turned round, screamed and ran up the steps. The deceased struggled to get away from Whittaker, who was in a carriage about three off the last one.

Mr Walmesley (representing the company) said: "We knew that the train would be down from Longridge about three o'clock. The gates are open about three minutes before the train arrives, for parties to go to the booking office, so that during that time anyone would be able to get to the platform space". Margaret Kay did not see the deceased put up her hand at all. She saw her go along the train for two or three yards. Her crinoline seemed to catch the train and then she fell. P.C. John Bennett said that he found her lying on the rails. "The train had gone over her head and also one of her legs and arm. She was quite dead at the time. I took her off the rails and into the station tavern and sent for a Doctor". The Coroner, in summing up, pointed out to the Jury that evidence was of a contradictory character and said that if Whittaker got hold of the girl's hand and stuck to it he would be guilty of manslaughter. A Verdict of Accidental Death was recorded".' [74]

Despite the verdict, Whittaker was subsequently charged with unlawful killing and, the following month, appeared at Preston Police (Magistrates) Court to undergo committal proceedings. The crucial evidence focused on whether Whittaker grabbed Maggie's hand first, in which case he would be guilty of manslaughter. Conversely, if the girl had held Whittaker's hand first, then he would not. Was it unlawful killing or accidental death? It transpired there was insufficient evidence to commit Whittaker for trial.

Enter the Maudland tunnel at your peril, for blood-curdling screams have been heard, from the girl in the crinoline dress who is said to haunt the oppressive and eerie blackness of the 'Miley tunnel', way beneath the busy streets of Preston.

The Sad Story of a Rag-and-Bone Man (1867)

An accident with dire consequences occurred at Grimsargh in 1867, when an inebriated fish hawker cum rag-and-bone man sustained fatal injuries while walking the line.

'It appears that a certain William Griffin of Snow Hill, Preston, was observed passing Grimsargh station rather the worse for liquor. The 5.30 pm express from Longridge, which does not stop until it reaches Preston, arrived within site of a bridge a quarter of a mile from Grimsargh station. (Preston Road overbridge) The engine driver noticed a man lying on the metals on the Preston side of the bridge. He blew the whistle, the brake was immediately applied and the engine reversed with full steam, but the engine and carriages passed over the man and was brought to a stand about 30 yards past the spot where he lay. Several persons alighted and, on examination, it was found that both legs had been severed from the body, the right arm was also cut off and the skull fractured. The unfortunate man lived about a quarter of an hour after the accident and could not articulate, although he appeared to understand what was said to him. How he had got on the line is not known. There is a fence and cutting 16 feet deep at this point. The body was removed to the Plough Inn at Grimsargh, there to await the inquest'. [75]

Train to Gammer Lane, for a Victorian Botanical Soirée at Red Scar in 1867

As a consequence of the PLR passenger service, there were new delights to be experienced and recreational pursuits to be enjoyed. Townsfolk joined the many Victorian clubs in Preston. Every town had its organised group of naturalists and naturally the local branch line had its own part to play. Members of the Preston Naturalists' Field Club discovered the great outdoors with a botanical walk to Red Scar from Gammer Lane Station (Fulwood Station) in July 1867: 'The Preston Naturalists' Field Club, which has recently been established at the Avenham Institution, made its first excursion on Wednesday afternoon.

There is no doubting the name of this station in this classic period photograph, although the name of the solitary staff member on the deserted platform is subject to conjecture. It was from this station that members of the Preston Naturalists' Field Club enjoyed a botanical walk to Red Scar in July 1867. Courtesy: Stephen Sartin

Going by rail to Gammer Lane station, they then walked towards Red Scar. On arriving at Red Scar, (about 2 miles) the party enjoyed the striking scenery there presented. The unique bend of the river with hanging woods along its margin, and the wide and varied landscape beyond make up a lovely natural picture ... Warned by gathering rain clouds, the excursionists cut short their intended visit to Brockholes Wood and returned by the Ribbleton moor. On passing over this well-known moor, which, before its enclosure, was esteemed the very paradise of local botanists, some of the party gathered fine specimens of the marsh gentian, a rare and beautiful plant, which is rapidly becoming extinct in the neighbourhood. The cross leaved heath and common heather were also picked up in the same place, making an aggregate of more than forty different plants, ferns and grasses, gathered in the course of the journey.' [76]

A Shock for the Signalman at Longridge in 1891

'On Wednesday evening a violent thunderstorm broke out over Longridge. A vivid flash of lightning followed immediately by a tremendous crash of thunder, created great alarm especially among a number of persons at Longridge Railway station who were waiting for a train to Preston. A large tree at the rear of the station was found to have been shattered, and the points man at the signal-box near the station was pulling one of the levers at the time of the flash and received an electric shock'. [77]

Cows on the Line in 1892

At Ribbleton and Grimsargh, there was once a countryside and wildlife haven representative of a forgotten Victorian landscape. An abundance of meadows and cornfields, gardens and orchards, was once the haunt of larks ascending, enigmatic corncrakes and tumbling lapwings and all to be occasionally enjoyed from the carriage window. Where urban expansion has now completely engulfed the countryside around the City of Preston, it is now hard to imagine that, in October 1892, the driver of the 2.20 p.m. train from Longridge to Preston noticed three cows on the tracks between Fulwood and Deepdale and was able stop just in time to avert a possible disaster.[78] This was, indeed, a landscape that witnessed the birth and boom of the Victorian railway age that was to transform the local communities at Ribbleton, Grimsargh and Longridge, which ultimately led to the urban expansion of Preston.

As a footnote could it have been however, that if the same driver had been able to cast his mind back to 1849, when animals shared first class compartments with other passengers, that he could have been forgiven for thinking that these particular beasts had simply missed the trian!

The engine crew would blow the engine's whistle long and hard on the approach to Stone Bridge in order to alert the signalman to open the gates in Berry Lane and to awaken the boss. Courtesy: Longridge & District Local History Society

Wedding Bells for the Station Master in 1892

'The station master, Mr W. Parr, was married on Wednesday, at Longridge Parish Church, to Miss E. Barnes. The Reverend Peter performed the ceremony and Mr Hindle of Darwen was best man. The newly-married pair left the station by the 12.15 p.m. train to Preston, amidst the booming of fog signals placed on the metals in honour of the event, and will be spending their honeymoon in Scotland. Mr Parr, who was formerly clerk-in-charge at Poulton station, was posted to his present position some three years ago'. [79]

A Requisitioned Whistle for the Boss, *c.* 1880

We end this potpourri of events with the dilemma faced by train crews in awakening the Secretary of the PLR, a fact alluded to by Tom Smith in his *History of Longridge*. 'Mr H.B. Jones was Secretary of the Longridge Railway for some years. He was an easy going man as the following instance shows: The engine driver had instructions always to whistle hard coming through the stone-bridge tunnel at Longridge, in order to waken the this somnolent official, and often enough the train had to come to a standstill, owing to the Secretary being in bed'.

CHAPTER SIX

'Grimsargh: Change for Whittingham!'

A One-way Ticket to Whittingham Hospital on the 'No Fare Train.'

Before moving onto twentieth century developments described in part two, the Victorian theme continues with a concise account of the single-track Whittingham Hospital Railway, especially with regard to its social and economic relevance to the PLR. A host of memories of Whittingham and its unique railway have stimulated the research for this chapter and provided the inspiration to share a further measure of Lancashire's social and railway history.

The associated Whittingham Hospital branch line was linked with the Preston to Longridge railway at Grimsargh for over half a century and to understand the origins of the hospital and its transport link it is fitting to focus on the prevailing social conditions in Preston at the height of the industrial revolution which led to the building of hospitals such as Whittingham, for the accommodation of paupers and the mentally ill.

During the Victorian era, Preston had been transformed into a town crammed with mills, terraced houses and cobbled streets. This was at the height of the Industrial Revolution, when 'King Cotton' reigned supreme, although there was little prosperity for certain factions. Disease and infant mortality were high among working-class families and the town was without piped water, drains or sewers, at a time when the number of unemployed peaked at 14,500 during April 1863, effectively reducing elements of the population to pauperism. It is therefore not surprising that Charles Dickens gained some inspiration for the Preston based novel, *Hard Times*, where his literary eye was focused on squalor and the appalling conditions which ultimately consigned certain of the populous to labour at the workhouse tread mill.

Two reports from 1865, in the wake of the infamous cotton famine, illustrate the level of extreme poverty, deprivation and vulnerability of young people: 'Congregations of all sorts of men, women and children are gathered in the thief's kitchen. In these places, lads, women, men, girls, beggars, thieves, tramps,

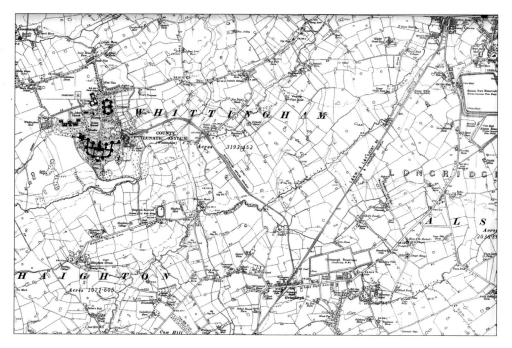

Edition of 1914 Ordnance Survey 6" to one mile map showing the complete Preston to Longridge railway and associated Whittingham Hospital branch.

vagabonds, cripples and prostitutes sleep together, without any respect to age or any distinction of sex, huddling in imperfectly ventilated rooms, and taking off their clothing before retiring to rest on account of the vermin. [80]

'The singing room we visited was up a flight of steps out of a stable yard, in a court not a hundred miles from the market place ... Can any good emanate from such places ... Little by little the girl loses her modesty, and the end is as sure and certain as is the clergyman's hope of her joyful resurrection after her life of vice with its daily battling with hunger, and her wretched death in the workhouse infirmary.' [81]

'The Regulation, Care and Treatment of Lunatics Act, 1845', required the provision of asylums for the care of pauper lunatics. Legislation in 1853 prohibited restraining devices on lunatics in workhouses, which led to pressure for the mentally ill to be fully institutionalised. At a time when facilities fell short of the demand for accommodation, it was decided to build a 1,000-bedded asylum at Whittingham, based on a house that was renamed St Luke's and work then commenced on the first of four main phases. St Luke's main building incorporated wards and a superb ballroom and, viewed from the front elevation, the building could easily have passed-off as one of the stately homes of England. Building materials were brought by road from Preston and Longridge. Bricks were made on-site; the source being what became an ornamental lake, one that is referred to on old maps as the 'fish pond'. It was not until 1873 that the first patients were admitted. The hospital was enlarged in 1879, to accommodate 2,895 patients and on 1 April 1893 the official opening took place.

Long before the era of motor vehicles and the established railway network, horse-drawn carts were used to convey supplies from Preston or Longridge Station to Whittingham. A proposed 'Whittingham Tramway' was first conceived in 1884, as a vital link with the outside world; henceforth, it would transport supplies of coal and hospital provisions from a new private station at Grimsargh. During the same year, a four-man committee was established at Whittingham, when it was estimated that the cost of the 2,863-yard standard-gauge line, at £12,000, would give an annual saving of £1,050 over road-haulage. However, this was conditional upon the LNWR and LYR Joint Ownership working the service. The company declined, but instead granted junction facilities with their 'main line' at Grimsargh. On 1 October 1884, application was made for a siding to connect the proposed asylum railway to Grimsargh Station. [82]

At the time of the railway being conceived, there was considerable wrangling at the hospital between the finance and general purposes committee and its four-man sub-committee. Following protracted exchanges within the hospital's boardroom, it was beginning to look like the whole concept of a railway was about to be thwarted. Further revision of the costs brought the estimated price down to £9,000, but the finance committee had still rejected the proposal. Undaunted, the sub-committee decided to circumvent internal dissension by applying the full might of the law and, in January 1885, the Annual Sessions at Preston presented a bill to parliament, which was duly approved. Although the finance committee conceded, it is likely that the sub-committee made certain concessions.

The original sub-committee became known as the 'Tramway Sub Committee'. Due to strong opposition from landowners, a period of two years elapsed before all the necessary land could finally be purchased. Railway archives from 1887 describe how, 'It was proposed to make a tramway. A plan of the junction has been prepared and it is proposed to carry out work, subject to county authorities paying the cost, and agreeing to pay the future expense and maintenance.' [83] The first sod was cut at Grimsargh in 1887 but construction work was delayed by wet and cold weather across difficult terrain. The severe winter of 1887 caused severe earth movements and the embankment near to Whittingham to slip. By 1888, the £9,000 allotted for the railway was almost spent. Application was then made to the Finance Committee for a further £5,000, which was needed to complete the works and to provide a locomotive and rolling stock, thus avoiding any need for horse traction. Extra funding was provided and, in March 1889, it was reported that the permanent way was finished, and traffic began running on the line in June of the same year.

The Victorian historian, Tom Smith, alluded to the opening of the Whittingham branch: 'A tramway has just been completed between the Asylum and Grimsargh

Station, on the Preston to Longridge railway line. We venture to hope that this tramway will, in a short time, be open to the people of Whittingham and Goosnargh, as in such a case the district will be largely developed ... The steam tram to Whittingham Asylum starts from Grimsargh; but costly as the venture had proved to the county ratepayers, the line is not allowed to be utilised by the public for local traffic – a state of affairs which doubtless the County Council will at once rectify for local traffic.'

The end of the Great War brought a change of name from Whittingham Asylum to Whittingham Mental Hospital and, by the outbreak of the Second World War, the patient population was 3,533, which made it the largest mental hospital in the country. Meanwhile, the diminutive train that slowly crossed over the level crossing in front of St Luke's main hospital building somehow completed the finishing touches and added to the allure of a remote establishment that seemed far apart from the twentieth century. Here was a community that seemed to have been lost in the mists of time, when the railway was the only contact with their outside world, and when patients and staff began to discover the mysteries of what lay beyond their parochial existance.

Veteran and Vintage Steam Locomotives and Stock

Surprisingly, throughout its sixty-eight year existence, the WHR aspired to only four hard-working steam locomotives and details are given below.

Builder	Class	Year Acquired	Acquired From	Year Disposed
A. Barclay	0-4-0	1888	A. Barclay	1946
-do-	0-4-2	1904	-do-	1952
W. Stroudley	D1 0-4-2T	1947	Southern Rly.	1955
Sentinel	0-4-0 WVBT	1953	Bolton Gasworks	1957

A brand-new 0-4-0 saddle-tank engine was the first locomotive to be purchased from Andrew Barclay and Sons, Kilmarnock, in 1888, for the sum of £790. At the same time, two goods vans were ordered to make up its train. The first four-wheel passenger carriage was purchased in 1889 for £277.10s from the Lancaster Carriage and Wagon Company. Not surprisingly, a single carriage proved to be inadequate for the number of passengers being transported. Therefore, in 1895 two former four-wheeled composite second and third class North London Railway carriages were purchased for £180 from the London & North Western Railway. The carriages were easily distinguished by a set of steps at either end, which gave access to the roof. These steps were used for maintenance and by the lamplighter to illuminate the carriage compartments. Thereafter, a total of three four-wheeled second hand carriages were purchased from the Lancashire and Yorkshire Railway, two in 1906 and one in 1910.

Although the Whittingham line was class-less the LYR carriages afforded a modicum of luxury, with roof lamps and cushioned seats. The compartments were still marked first, second and third, a legacy of the previous owners, for no money was ever exchanged for tickets on the hospital railway. When the PLR passenger service ceased in 1930, the original red and white-liveried carriages were reduced to three, perhaps an indication that there was less of a demand for the Whittingham service.

The carriage stock lasted until 1946, when they were ignominiously shunted into a running loop near Whittingham Station and left to rot. They were replaced by three converted ex-LNWR 20-ton goods brake vans, complete with side seats round the carriage interior and five small windows for added passenger comfort. Calor Gas was installed for cold winter journeys, the containers being neatly padlocked inside the coaches.

A second Barclay 0-4-2-side tank was purchased from Andrew Barclay and Sons, Kilmarnock in 1904 to join its sister engine on the Whittingham line and between the two world wars, the two Barclays were the sole motive power on the line. Regular drivers and firemen manned them. On 27 March 1927, Mr John Titley of Longridge applied for, and was offered, a post as driver. A letter from the Medical Superintendent at Whittingham Hospital set out his terms of reference:

During the first decades of the twentieth century the passenger accommodation was provided in ex-Lancashire and Yorkshire and North London carriages (the latter with steps at either end). These carriages bore the letters CAW up to 1923 and CMHW thereafter. Courtesy: Alan Summerfield

The original 0-4-0 Barclay No. 1 of 1888 pauses between trips at Grimsargh Station. Courtesy: George Whiteman

Barclay No. 1 approaching Whittingham with a mixture of classic veteran carriages. Courtesy: George Whiteman Collection

Barclay No. 1 crossing over Brabiner Lane Bridge on the approach to Whittingham. Courtesy: George Whiteman Collection

Barclay 0-4-2 No. 2 leaves Grimsargh Station with original carriage stock around the time of the Great War. Courtesy: Mrs Frances Wright

Barclay No. 2 at Grimsargh Station. The original veteran carriages were superseded by these three green converted ex-LNWR guard's vans in 1946. Courtesy: Alan Summerfield

In March 1956, Barclay No. 2 approaches Whittingham Station, on a high embankment, with a passenger train. Courtesy: Alan Summerfield

'Dear Sir,

With reference to your application for the post of locomotive driver here: We can offer you the post and the vacancy will take place during next month, the exact date will be given you later on. The wages will be £4.5.8d per week (55 hours) Will you please inform us per return of post whether you accept the situation.

Yours faithfully, Medical Superintendent.' [84]

Mr Titley duly accepted the post as driver and, earning a modest wage, he nurtured the two Barclays for fourteen years. Mr Gilbert Wright, who was to drive the very last steam engine along the line in 1957, succeeded Mr Titley as driver in 1942.

Technical Details of the Barclay Locomotives

Barclay No. 1 (0-4-0 saddle-tank)	Barclay No. 2 (0-4-2 side-tank)
Works number – 304	Works number – 1026
Date purchased – 1888	Date purchased – 1904
Cylinders 13" x 20"	Cylinders 13" x 20"
Coupled wheels 3' 7" diameter	4' 1" diameter, trailing 3' 0" diameter.
Boiler – working pressure 120lbs/sq. in	Boiler – working pressure 160 lbs/sq. in
Heating surface – boiler 440 sq. feet	Heating surface – boiler 460 sq. feet
Heating surface – firebox 48 sq. feet	Heating surface – firebox 52 sq. feet
Tank capacities 640 gallons of water	Tank capacities 640 gallons of water
Weight loco. Empty 19 ton 5 cwt	Weight loco. Empty 21 ton 5 cwt
Weight loco. Loaded 23 ton 5 cwt	Weight loco. Loaded 25 ton

With the demise of Barclay No. 1 in 1946, a replacement engine was urgently sought. Approaches to the railway companies were made for a suitable machine and only the Southern Railway responded, with the offer of a Stroudley 0-4-2 (T) class D1, originally No. 357. Up to the 1920s, such engines worked on London suburban lines but, as electrification developed, most of the survivors were fitted for push-and-pull working in country areas. In February 1947, the D1 was purchased for Whittingham at a cost of £750, for immediate operational use as CMHW No. 1. This acquisition coincided with pre-nationalisation, when many veterans of the 'iron road' were destined for scrap. When the engine arrived at Whittingham, it still bore the southern nameplate of Riddlesdown, and the words 'Southern Railway'. The locomotive, withdrawn in 1944, was even older than the line, having been manufactured in 1886 and, not surprisingly, it was the sole survivor of its class.

In October 1947, during a ceremony at Whittingham Hospital Station, the locomotive was named 'James Fryars', in honour of Alderman Fryar, Chairman of the hospital visiting committee. Amidst clouds of steam from his namesake engine, Alderman Fryar, gave a brief history of the railway to the assembled committee including Mr W. A. Higgs (hospital management) who explained: 'In addition to ten double journeys each day, hauling passenger trains the locomotive will be used for bringing vital goods traffic to the hospital. An average of 12,000 tons of coal and slack is brought along the railway from Grimsargh each year, as well as hundreds of tons of other goods. The passenger service is entirely free, and carries more than 200 of the hospital staff to and from Grimsargh daily. The service is also used by visitors to patients at the hospital.' Alderman Fryar stated, 'Three brake vans have been acquired from the LMS and are now fitted out as passenger carriages.'

With Driver Whalley and Fireman Young 'up front' on the footplate, he then led the committee for a guided tour of the line to Grimsargh, but afterwards, Fireman Young said: 'Jimmy Fryar's all right on the straight, but she grinds a bit on the bends.' The locomotive was said to be so powerful that the regulator needed minimal opening throughout the journey. The journey time from Grimsargh to Whittingham Station depended on the capability of the particular locomotive. The D1 took on average about six minutes to complete the journey, though it was well capable of doing the journey in three to four minutes.

Class D1 Stroudly 0-4-2, side tank originally No. 357 (later 2357), formerly worked on the London, Brighton and South Coast Railway. It is seen here at New Cross Gate on 8 October 1938. Courtesy: HCC/RMC

The D1 at Guildford on 3 September 1932, as Southern, No. 2357. The engine was transferred to Whittingham in 1947. Courtesy: HCC/RMC

The D1 'James Fryars', by now in WHR green livery with nameplate above the inscription CMHW No. 1, pauses at Whittingham on 1 May 1954. Viewed from any angle, the engine made an alluring sight. Courtesy: R. H. Hughes, Manchester Locomotive Society

Above and below: On a visit to the WHR by Mr H. Casserley and his son Richard on 21 April 1951, the D1 Stroudley dragged the Barclay 0-4-2 out of the engine shed to be photographed. Courtesy: HCC/RMC

The D1 0-6-2 on its arrival at Whittingham Station with an enthusiasts' special on 1 May 1954.
Courtesy: R. H. Hughes, Manchester Locomotive Society

Whittingham engine shed with the boiler of the Stroudley standing forlornly and ultimately destined
for scrap. Courtesy: N. Evans Collection

The D1 was to survive for less than ten years, for, by 1955, the engine was suffering from serious boiler problems and there was no one to perform major surgery at the hospital in respect of a condemned boiler! Consequently, about two years before the Whittingham line closed, the engine took a one-way ticket to a siding and stood forlornly outside the shed in terminal decline.

Following the demise of Barclay No. 2 in 1952, a replacement engine was urgently sought. It transpired that in 1953 a driver was instructed to 'go to Bolton Gas-works to pick up an engine.' The fourth and final acquisition had been built at Sentinel wagon works, Shrewbury in 1947, works number 9377, as a 0-4-0 Sentinel 100 hp steam engine. In fact, 'Gradwell' was still resplendent with the emblem of Bolton Corporation on the dummy boiler casing. The vertical water-tube boiler was in the cab. The diminutive engine was capable of hauling the three passenger carriages without effort, or up to about thirty twelve-ton wagons, weighing around 360 tons. With a modest running speed of only thirteen miles an hour, 'Gradwell' operated the service almost single-handed during the final year of the railway's existence and just about maintained the status quo.

Following complete closure of the WHR on 29 June 1957, the Sentinel gained pastures new in north-east England when sold to Messrs G. Stephenson, builders and contractors of Bishop Auckland, who in turn resold it in 1958 to the Tyne Tees Shipping Company of Stockton-on-Tees, where it later worked at Vulcan Street Wharf in Middlesbrough. The engine had been given a new lease of life, but was finally scrapped in 1968, eleven years after departure from the Whittingham line.

'Gradwell' with special train at Grimsargh on 1 June 1957. Courtesy: N. Evans Collection

'Gradwell' letting off steam in the picturesque grounds of Whittingham Hospital on 1 June 1957.
Courtesy: N. Evans Collection

'James Fryars' joins sister engine 'Gradwell' on the shed road at Whittingham on 1 May 1954.
Courtesy: R. H. Hughes, Manchester Locomotive Society

A rare image of 'Gradwell' with a coal train heading from Grimsargh to Whittingham. Courtesy: N. Evans Collection

Following closure of the line in 1957, the remains of the iconic D1 locomotive were sold for scrap for a mere £350. With hindsight, if only we had known then what we know now! The unfortunate loss of the Stroudley preceded the railway preservation era, though it was as a direct result of the loss of such locomotives and branch lines in the 1960s that the heritage railway movement was born and, with it, the acquisition of redundant locomotives and former branch lines.

Basic Facilities and Operations

The Grimsargh to Whittingham line was precisely one mile four furlongs and 9.7 chains long and was originally constructed to convey coal and provisions to the new hospital from the joint London & North Western and Lancashire & Yorkshire's Preston to Longridge branch line at Grimsargh. In the overall scheme of events, the passenger service emerges as something of an afterthought and one for which basic facilities were provided. Henceforth it became known as the nurses' special because it conveyed hospital staff working shifts who resided in Preston and Ribbleton, as well as the surrounding villages of Grimsargh, Longridge, Chipping and Ribchester. Indeed, anyone could travel free of charge on the 'no fare train,' and even before the dawn of railway preservation its fame spread far and wide.

Both Grimsargh and Whittingham Stations were precursors to the un-staffed halts of today and remained permanently un-manned throughout their existence. Grimsargh Station exemplified a period country branch bay terminus, complete with a run-round loop, a connection with the PLR and two sidings to facilitate

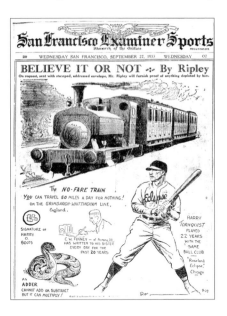

Amazingly, Barclay No. 1 found fame in San Francisco where it evidently appealed to devotees of railway history. This drawing of the Whittingham train featured in the *San Francisco Examiner* on 27 September 1933. The caption read: 'No fare train. You can travel fifty miles a day for nothing on the Grimsargh to Whittingham line, England.'

freight interchange. The station platform was originally 40 ft in length by 12 ft wide, with a 10 ft waiting room. In 1918, during the peak of passenger services, the platform was transformed into a substantial structure 218 ft long and remained in this form until the line closed in 1957. The connection to the Longridge branch was worked from a ground-frame released by an Annett's key placed in the frame, to enable shunting or traffic movement.

At the time of the opening of the line, the first Whittingham Station occupied the site of the engine-shed that was then at the end of the line. A new Whittingham Station was built around 1907 for approximately £500, the undertaking being funded by the Lancashire Asylums Board. The station's construction comprised brick and iron pillars supporting an overall glass roof about 150 ft long, which also served as a carriage shed. Steps led up onto a narrow single wooden platform and to a brick waiting room. The curvature alongside the platform was said to be so sharp that it restricted the use of bogie carriages.

The WHR owed its origins to the carrying of fossil fuels to the hospital's gas-works and boiler-house. The gas-works and boiler-house were respectively situated at the western and eastern extremities of the hospital's grounds. On entering Whittingham station yard, wagons were separately weighed before being authorised to proceed to the respective power plants.

An examination of the 25-inch to one mile Ordnance Survey map on page 127 reveals the track layout in the hospital grounds and clarifies that a gas-works was linked by rail. The route is shown leading from the station yard via a complex of buildings to the gas-works. Owing to restricted space between buildings, two short turntables were installed for wagons to be turned through an angle of ninety degrees. Wagons were then propelled to the gas-works.

Grimsargh WHR Station with two prospective passengers. The run round loop also features with mixed freight stock in the siding beyond. Courtesy: HCC/RMC

Whittingham Station and weighbridge office (right foreground), where the line forked to the engine shed, sidings and the hospital grounds. Courtesy: HCC/RMC

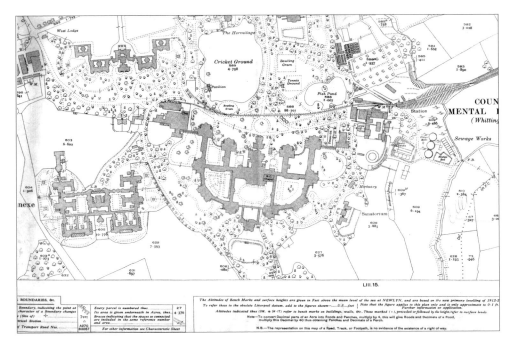

The 25-inch to one mile Ordnance Survey map of Whittingham Hospital, illustrating the extension of the railway that ran through the hospital grounds. Courtesy: Lancashire County Council

Beyond Whittingham Station, the line crossed landscaped lawns and gardens that led to the boiler house. Courtesy: HCC/RMC

'James Fryars' passes alongside the lake in the grounds of Whittingham Hospital with a special train for enthusiasts, on 1 May 1954. Courtesy: R. H. Hughes, Manchester Locomotive Society

The single-road engine-shed could accommodate two steam engines and was provided with appropriate machinery for the hospital's engineers. It did, however, lack such basic facilities as a water tower and it appears that, instead, a hosepipe was used. At first, coaling the engine was done the hard way, with plenty of muscle power and good old Lancashire elbow grease. Latterly, the crew enjoyed the luxury of a conveyor-belt that shifted the coal direct from a commodious coal dump to the steam engine's bunker. Typically, it was a case of 'make do and mend,' with limited resources and second-hand materials being invariably obtained and adapted for a change of use.

The centre-road led to the engine-shed siding and through the picturesque hospital grounds to the boiler-house. It was only in 1922 that the line was extended 520 yards through the grounds to a new boiler-house, at a cost of £3,200. The project included a short siding that was used for shunting coal wagons to a reserve supply of coal situated near the cricket field. Apart from special trains run for enthusiasts, passenger trains from Grimsargh never went beyond Whittingham Station, as the extension was for goods trains only. The additional track to the boiler-house provided a total length of 3,386 yards (3,096 metres) from Grimsargh Station.

Throughout the hospital grounds, special precautions had to be taken to protect the public and patients from oncoming trains. Engine crews had to remain especially vigilant and to keep ceaseless watch for vehicles and pedestrians crossing the line, which necessitated the trains moving very slowly and the fireman preceding the locomotive as a walking pilot. Sadly, in September 1894, a train near Whittingham Station struck a male patient who sustained fatal injuries. Four years later, a hospital patient committed suicide on the Whittingham Line.

The passenger service on the line was beginning to reach fruition towards the end of the Victorian era. During its 1918 heyday, the Whittingham train carried about 3,000 passengers per week and more than 12,000 tons of freight per annum. Throughout its existence, trains were often mixed, with goods and passenger vehicles running together. There were twelve daily passenger trains operating in each direction, the first leaving Whittingham at 6.10 a.m. and the final departure from Grimsargh at 9.35 p.m. Extra trains ran on Saturdays for the visitors, but in all probability there was never a Sunday or Bank Holiday service. At the time of peak operations, it was not uncommon for the train to carry 200 passengers on Saturday afternoons. The extra traffic generated by the WHR boosted freight and passenger traffic on the PLR, which, in turn, was an essential feeder to the Whittingham line.

During the Second World War, the locomotives, stock and track infrastructure degenerated and, in 1947, 1,048 yards of track were re-laid and 1,798 yards of track re-sleepered, at a cost of £7,050. Major work on the permanent way combining the partial re-laying of sleepers and rail was also undertaken at the time that the line was extended in 1922, again in 1930 and for the last time in 1952. The track was generally maintained in good condition and had checkrails on the severe curves. Some of the sidings were not replaced and the seven hundred feet long loop near Whittingham Station, installed around 1912, appears to have been the oldest part of the line.

After the war, the provision of a direct Ribble bus service from Preston to Whittingham led to a reduction in passengers and, consequently, the 1951 timetable mirrors a decline in services on the line, although extra trains were still provided on Saturday afternoons for hospital visitors.

Grimsargh to Whittingham (weekdays)	Whittingham to Grimsargh (weekdays)
6.35am, 7.30am, 8.40am, 12.30pm, 1.30pm (SO), 2.30pm (SO), 5.20pm, 6.30pm, 7.20pm.	6.10am, 7.10am, 8am, 11.50am (SO), 1.7pm (SO), 1.30pm (SX), 2pm (SO), 4.35pm (SO), 5pm (SX), 5.40pm, 7.10pm.

During the quiet morning period, the timetable made provision for the daily freight train, which left Whittingham at approximately 10.00 a.m. with empty goods wagons and usually returned from Grimsargh at 11.30 a.m. with loaded coal wagons. An ex-Midland Railway freight van was also provided for the carrying of hospital provisions and other goods.

Up to 1951, a primitive system of push-and-pull working operated on the WHR Passenger trains were always hauled from Grimsargh to Whittingham. As there was no station loop or turntable at Whittingham yard, it was the practice for the engine to propel the train back to Grimsargh from the rear of the train.

This method led to the Whittingham train having an unsavoury reputation with local farmers and livestock, especially when an accident occurred on 2 September 1950. Several occupation crossings provided the way for cattle to be brought across the permanent way twice daily for milking, but the serenity of the idyllic countryside was shattered when a train hit three exuberant heifers that had wandered onto the track from the crossing serving Brabiner House Farm. One beast was killed outright and the other two had to be destroyed. The farmer claimed damages and a County Court Judge made certain recommendations that henceforth all trains should be hauled in both directions plus incorporated turn-round facilities at Whittingham. On this most basic of railway lines it seemed to be a question of making use of limited resources and at first this was achieved by the judicious use of a towrope. In later years, the marvels of modern technology were invoked with the installation of a hoover like contraption known as a BSA 'wagon mover.'

This ingenious equipment was petrol driven and had handlebars and rubber wheels that ran on one rail with the crew walking alongside and controlling its movement. Not surprisingly, the noisy contraption is now an exhibit at the National Railway Museum. Running round the train was then achieved by uncoupling the engine that was at the head of the train arriving from Grimsargh. While the engine entered the shed road for service the fireman produced the motorised pusher and drove it along the rails until it coupled with the carriage. The fireman then engaged the clutch of the wagon mover and pushed the three carriages into the carriage road to enable the engine to regain its rightful place at the head of the train. In future, the driver would enjoy his Sunday joint of roast beef with a clear conscience, without the fear of having sent curious bovines to the knacker's yard!

The End of the Line

It transpired that, by 1956, following the withdrawal of the D1 locomotive, a replacement engine to work alongside 'Gradwell' was inconceivable. Consequently, it was with some sadness and reluctance on the part of the Whittingham Hospital Management Committee that a decision was made to close the line as from January 1957. Although the railway was said to be conveying some 200 hospital employees each day, loading was down to single figures on certain journeys, with only one carriage being used. The railway cost about £5,000 per annum to run and road haulage of coal direct to the hospital's boilers was considered to be more cost effective. However, owing to the Suez crisis and consequential petrol rationing, hospital management waited for the international crisis to subside and in the interim gave the line two reprieves, but this only stalled the inevitable closure.

On 1 June 1957, sixty enthusiasts, on a farewell tour sponsored by three locomotive societies, visited the Whittingham line. Two return trips were made with 'Gradwell' at the head of the train, which consisted of the three passenger brake vans and two open wagons adapted for passengers. Stranger than fiction, in these days of health and safety awareness and perhaps the only place in the world where the passenger trains were regularly hauled by an unorthodox geared Sentinel locomotive – yet another first for this unique line.

Throughout June, 'Gradwell' was draped with bunting, culminating in a commemorative special train for VIPs on 27 June. On this auspicious occasion the proud little engine carried a special board in front of the boiler proclaiming its heritage –'Whittingham Railway 1887-1957.' The very last scheduled passenger train, hauled by 'Gradwell', ran from Grimsargh to Whittingham at 7.20 p.m. on 29 June 1957. I remember there was hardly any ceremony on that June evening, only a prevailing feeling of sadness for a small group of about twenty nurses, relatives of the train crew and 'yours truly.' As Driver Gilbert Wright opened the regulator and blew a melancholy whistle on the 7.20 p.m. to Whittingham, the Sentinel steam engine chugged away into history. The event was, however, modestly commemorated by several fog signals that simultaneously exploded on the single track, by now woven into the pleasant undulating landscape of Lancashire, but sadly for not much longer.

'Gradwell' had earned accolades from the crews for its speed of steam raising, enabling the fire to be dropped every night. At this time the fire was to be lit on just a few more occasions; while 'Gradwell' was temporarily engaged on track demolition between Grimsargh and Whittingham, no doubt a very heart-rending experience for driver Gilbert Wright, who had fulfilled this last duty by 1958. The Sentinel gained pastures new in north-east England when sold to Messrs G. Stephenson, builders and contractors of Bishop Auckland, who in turn resold it in 1958 to the Tyne Tees Shipping Company of Stockton-on-Tees, where it later worked at Vulcan Street Wharf in Middlesbrough. The engine was finally scrapped in 1968, eleven years after departure from the Whittingham line.

Today, a few scars left on the landscape and a black corroded iron fence belie the course of the railway. Footpath crossings and stiles still give access to the track-bed, where agricultural land now reaches out across to reclaim the former railway. After closure, the tracks were removed and the land was sold and reclaimed. The bridge over Brabiner Lane lasted until demolition in 1978 and a stone-arched bridge still survives intact at Dale Brow, near to Brabiner Lane, where certain earthworks over the middle section remain intact. Both stations have long since disappeared. Whittingham Hospital itself was closed completely on 31 March 1995, and most of the complex has now been demolished.

While walking across the old track bed at Dixon's Farm, Grimsargh, I well recall that evening of 29 June 1957, with dream-like images of a hissing snake-like train writhing away round the double bends lodged in my psyche. Into the sunset it went for the very last time, recalling a bygone railway age that had existed since Victorian times.

'Gradwell' is draped with bunting in preparation for the last journey on the 7.20 p.m. from Grimsargh to Whittingham on 29 June 1957. Driver Gilbert Wright is on the footplate (complete with young admirer) while Fireman Bennett waits on the platform. Courtesy: Mrs Frances Wright

This atmospheric photograph portrays 'Gradwell' on the last journey to Whittingham on Saturday 29 June 1957, suitably adorned with headboard encapsulating the line's history. Photograph: Dr G. P. Reed MB (Medical Officer British Railways)

The derelict shell of the handsome St Luke's main hospital building at Whittingham Hospital, awaiting demolition in 2008. David Hindle

Alongside a completely overgrown track-bed are several concrete blocks that once formed the base of Whittingham Station. David Hindle

Today, this iron fence at Grimsargh represents the course of the WHR. David Hindle

A Nostalgic Footplate Ride on 'James Fryars.'

The focus now turns to my own lasting impressions of a train journey along the line at some imprecise date lost in the 'mists of time.' I knew Grimsargh in the early 1950s, when the main Preston Road was obstructed twice a day by the closing of the level-crossing gates situated between the two stations. As the tired old L&YR 0-6-0 steam engine prepared to show its true colours in tackling the ascent to Longridge, a veteran locomotive with a combination of up to three green passenger carriages bearing an uncanny resemblance to horseboxes, gently simmered in Grimsargh's second railway station.

My grandfather first introduced me to the delights of the Whittingham line with a ride on his BSA Bantam to Grimsargh Station. There we discovered a waiting room with a roaring coal fire and a single electric light bulb but not a single person in sight. It was rather like the *Marie Celeste*, a ghost station with no staff. From the long station platform we suddenly witnessed a bizarre occurrence. Beneath considerable smoke emissions, an ancient steam engine suddenly appeared around the curve close to Dixon's Farm. As the apparition drew nearer, along rails deeply submerged in a weedy single-track, the sight and sound of steam was instantly perceived. Upon arrival and after running round its train, I stood in awe at the sight of a truly antiquated steam engine named 'James Fryars' while witnessing the shift of hospital workers slamming the doors of the three green carriages.

It was then that the kindly engine crew allowed me on the footplate to look at the fiery furnace that was at the heart of the impressive engine, affectionately known by driver Wright and fireman Bennet as 'Jimmy Fryar'. The two engine crews worked from about 5 a.m. to 1 p.m. and 1 p.m. to 9 p.m. respectively and turns were exchanged on alternate weeks with driver Whalley and fireman Dunn. Meanwhile, to my astonishment, fireman Bennett produced a coal shovel, which was placed above the roaring fire to fry bacon, eggs and mushrooms for breakfast. I am not too sure about the coal dust, but the locally picked giant field mushrooms on toast, washed down with tea from of the driver's 'billy can,' tasted delicious.

I suffered no ill effects from the mushrooms and we boarded the train. The patented coaches even had the luxury of wooden seats around the sides of the carriage and gas central heating provided by a Calor Gas bottle. About six windows allowed passengers to enjoy the picturesque countryside during the six-minute journey to Whittingham. Suddenly and unannounced there was a jolt and a lurch followed by a blow on the engine's whistle, as the train eased off from the platform to commence the journey to Whittingham. The driver had no need to worry about signals or single line tokens, because on this line they did not exist and who had ever heard of gradient or milepost signs? It was a fairly comfortable ride, at a speed of around 15-20 miles per hour.

There were no intermediate stations, merely a few unscheduled stops. If the old engine ran out of steam, or perhaps between flexible train times, opportunities often arose for train crews to gather mushrooms from the fields, or to collect wild flowers growing profusely in the cutting next to the line. During the untroubled glory days of the Whittingham line it was indeed funny old trains that helped to characterise the local landscape. This was at a time when the pastoral landscape between Grimsargh and Whittingham was augmented during haymaking time with a work force armed with swishing scythes and plenty of muscle and energy. Sadly, the rich tapestry of Grimsargh's luscious countryside and the scent of new-mown hay are long gone.

From Grimsargh Station, the line curved in a northwesterly direction away from the Longridge line, alongside a siding before reducing to single track approaching Dixon's Farm. Next to the farm, a family group gave us a friendly wave from a footpath that crossed the line and as we rode past flocks of lapwings and curlews and galloping heifers I became mesmerized by the whole experience of the Whittingham line, while observing that the frisky heifers had a clear lead over the engine and seemed to be winning an impromptu race. Advancing along a straight downward gradient, the train gained some speed and may even have reached 20 miles per hour – perish the thought – while crossing the valley of Savick Brook. The train then entered a cutting about 30-40 ft deep, gloriously festooned with wild flowers.

There was not a single bridge over the Whittingham line, only occupation/footpath crossings and culverts over Savick and Blundell Brooks. The largest structures on the line were two arched stone bridges, the first crossing over Brabiner Lane, and the second an occupation bridge bisecting fields near Dale Brow. Brabiner Lane Bridge was a particularly good example of skew bridge construction. This was where my parents took me in Dad's old Morris 8 to watch the train crossing over this minor country lane. While we were enjoying a picnic beside Blundell Brook, a plume of white smoke suddenly emerged from a cutting and the train passed by. The old car harmonised well with the country scene, enhanced by a cacophony of sound from the soft exhaust and shrill whistle of the engine to joyful chirrupy swallows and strident calls of curlews, echoing over the meadows.

Back on the train the familiar water tower landmark at Whittingham hospital came into view and, as the train trundled along, it seemed to acquire an unnerving swaying motion while negotiating a left hand curve on a high embankment. Approaching Whittingham Station, on a rising gradient of 1 in 120, the line passed an abandoned loop line, formerly used to store a collection of antiquated passenger carriages. The station commanded a panoramic view of the Bowland fells, though marred by the lingering perceptions of the hospital's sewage farm – not a real showstopper as tourist attractions go! Alighting from the train onto the narrow platform we walked past the engine-shed and around an ornamental lake in the hospital grounds. Then, after being attacked by a busking mute swan it was time to walk back to the railway station and experience the return journey to Grimsargh.

Grandad Bowman on his BSA motor bike. Photo: David Hindle

An almost deserted Grimsargh Station with the Sentinel and its single carriage epitomising the rural branch line. T. Heginbotham Collection

Grimsargh Station, showing the D1 Stroudley 0-4-2 with its train of converted brake vans about to depart from Grimsargh Station on 21 April 1951; lost somewhere in the mists of time wondrous journey behind this veteran locomotive to Whittingham and back. Courtesy: HCC/RMC

Shortly after leaving Grimsargh Station, 'James Fryars' passes the connecting link with the Longridge branch and heads for Whittingham in April 1952. Courtesy: Alan Summerfield

The elaborate Whittingham Station, with two waiting passengers on 1 May 1954. Courtesy: Gordon Biddle Collection – photograph by D. Thompson

The 'push me, pull you' train – 'James Fryars' is seen propelling its train from Whittingham to Grimsargh on 25 June 1952. Courtesy: Gordon Biddle

I look back with feelings of misgivings of that day and over lost opportunities to observe and photograph the golden days of steam. The smoke that drifted over the fields, accompanied by the shrill whistle and exhaust blasts of the labouring Whittingham engine, contrasted with the charismatic calls of lapwings, curlews and skylarks. Today, such quintessential elements of avian excellence are in rapid decline and the dearth of farmlands birds makes a compelling environmental statement. To a certain extent, a similar analogy might be applied to the network of local railways that were once pivotal to the rural landscape of England. A lament, perhaps, for the passing of nature and a way of community life that now seems long gone.

Brief Encounters

Research has revealed yet more anecdotal material and personal recollections of the line. The WHR was operated under the control of the Chief Mechanical Engineer at Whittingham but, on occasions, wayward trains required a degree of supervision, from the imagined fat controller. All of this sounds somewhat familiar and the Reverend W. Audrey would probably have gained further inspiration for his writings of *Thomas the Tank Engine* books, had he visited Whittingham.

Throughout the Edwardian era, road transport had yet to make its impact as a serious competitor for the railway. However, who would have thought of congestion problems at Grimsargh, caused by the asylum railway, as early as 1904? Grimsargh Parish Council resolved, 'That the clerk should write to the railway company pointing out the delay to traffic, through closing the gates on the level crossing adjoining Grimsargh station, and the measure of time taken by shunting operations on the asylum railway. Some attention is given to stop what at present is a great public nuisance.'

The fat controller was called upon in June 1926, when Grimsargh Parish Council presided over the serious incidence of the smoke and coal dust from the Whittingham Asylum train. The Barclay engine seemed to be beyond control, as it stood in the bay platform at Grimsargh after being stoked up, while waiting its next turn of duty. Clearly, something had to be done to address the problems of black blemishes smudging white sheets floating on washing lines: 'It was resolved: that the clerk should write to those in charge to fire the train up outside the station.'

The vagaries of the WHR timetable depended on the driver, who knew his passengers so well that if anyone missed the train, he would reverse the engine to the station to pick them up. For the occupiers of Dixon's farm, closure of the line in June 1957 was tinged with sadness and fond memories. When Ada Wild was a little girl, the kindly engine crew gave her a footplate lift from Grimsargh to an unscheduled stop at her home, Dixon's farm.

As the memories come flooding back, retired Wing Commander Alan Wilding shared with me his own recollections of the Whittingham line: 'I remember, as a small boy in the 1930s, that we set off for a trip on the small steam train, which then plied between Grimsargh and Whittingham Mental Hospital, for a walk in the hospital's grounds and to see a pantomime in the hospital ballroom. This was my first ever train ride and the train trip was the real object of the visit. I recall

Close up photographs of Barclay No. 2, complete with a corroded chimney and the letters CMHW No. 2. Courtesy: George Whiteman Collection

Barclay No. 2 departs Grimsargh and negotiates Whittingham Junction and begins the two mile journey to Whittingham Hospital along the floristic overgrown single track. Courtesy: George Whiteman Collection

'Gradwell' in the grounds of Whittingham Hospital. Courtesy: N. Evans Collection

that the service was used for a few passengers and bulk freight to the hospital.'

A 96-year-old retired nurse at Whittingham was a regular passenger on both the Whittingham and Longridge lines. The venerable gentleman described that in LMS days the trains from Preston and Deepdale were crowded with nurses who had to change at Grimsargh for the Whittingham train.

For the occupiers of Dixon's farm, closure of the line in June 1957 was tinged with sadness and fond memories. Gentlemen patients from Whittingham often 'walked the line' and enjoyed a kind welcome at the farm. One patient came into the house, made himself comfortable with a cup of tea, and asked if he might have a wash before walking back to the hospital. Another regular visitor was an elderly gentleman who had no known family. This lonely figure regularly walked to the 'windmill pit', where he spent many happy hours fishing before rounding off his day with a cup of tea at the farm, and walking back along the track to Whittingham.

Many Grimsargh people enjoyed the free rides and reminisce about watching the Christmas pantomimes staged in the ballroom, or spending a summer's evening enjoying cricket matches and walking round the lake, while having a chat with the friendly patients and staff. Love blossomed for quite a few Grimsargh couples within the precincts of Grimsargh's railway station and a parallel line could be drawn with the famous film, *Brief Encounter*.

When Trevor Howard met Celia Johnson at Carnforth railway station, there began a little nefarious activity, outwardly innocent. *Brief Encounter* was filmed against a background of those wonderful LMS locomotives, thundering through Carnforth Station. The renowned station café typically served mugs of tea, plastic facsimile cheese and limp tomato sandwiches. Here, to the accompaniment of Rachmaninov's second piano concerto, a brief encounter progressed favourably, especially when Trevor took his newly found lady friend to the local cinema. When the station clock called time on their flirtations it was time to walk the subway, before catching trains home to respective spouses and presumably they all lived happily ever after!

By contrast, Grimsargh never had a cinema and villagers did not need romantic music or double seats, evidenced by fond memories of Grimsargh's senior citizens, who recalled their courting days. It seems that after departure of the last train of the day to Whittingham, many late night branch line manoeuvres took place under Grimsargh's station canopy. Indeed, if David Lean had been on location his film would never have got past the censors. It is perhaps reassuring that the identities of the leading players will never reach the public domain.

Finally, a more tranquil scenario is that the railway scene between Grimsargh and Whittingham saw minimal change for almost seventy years and preserved the rustic essence of the railway and magnetism of this unique country branch line. There are spurious claims that a Whittingham engine was buried on site, although, in my view, tangible evidence is almost certainly lacking until, that is, someone discovers the Holy Grail! What is not in dispute is that had the Whittingham line survived, it would have become a 'mecca' for railway enthusiasts from far and wide. Gone but not entirely forgotten!

PART TWO

THE PLR IN THE TWENTIETH CENTURY

CHAPTER SEVEN

The Heyday of Freight and Passenger Services

Part two describes the crucial socio/economic events determining the rise and fall of the PLR between around 1900 and the complete closure of the last surviving segment of the line in 1994. The period under review in chapter seven covers the Joint LNWR and L&YR administration from the beginning of the twentieth century until the L&YRs amalgamation with the LNWR as from 1 January 1922, and the subsequent Grouping of the London Midland and Scottish Railway Company (LMS) in 1923.

A change of management from the Preston & Longridge Joint Committee to the LNWR and L&YR Joint Committee in 1889, probably contributed to greater prosperity for the PLR prior to the LMS Grouping in 1923. Corresponding with national trends, the passenger service peaked during the first two decades of the twentieth century. Timetable analysis for joint ownership between 1888 and 1911, LNWR ownership in 1922 and LMS ownership in 1929 indicate the pinnacle of passenger services which culminated with up to eleven weekday trains in 1922. By 1929 the service had been reduced to nine passenger trains on weekdays, ten on Saturdays and only one morning and one afternoon train on Sundays. It was chiefly the advent of rival bus companies that led to the complete withdrawal of regular passenger services in 1930.

During the latter half of joint administration the PLR became the province of LNWR Webb 2-4-2 tank engines working the passenger trains; however, they had limitations on the steep gradients and hence the need for occasional double heading of long excursion trains. A regular stock of four coaches became designated as the 'Preston-Longridge set.' Corridor coaches were not used for suburban services, tender engines were not needed, and it was for this reason that the company used tank engines for passenger workings and this type of coaching stock.

A new experimental motor train made its debut on the PLR in 1914, and in order to facilitate turn round operations at either end of the line it operated as a push-and-pull train. The new train was duly reviewed in the *Preston Guardian* on 9 May 1914:

Preston to Longridge

PRESTON	615	9 0	11 0	1220	135	...		5 3	613	830	1040			930	3 5	830
Deepdale	62c	9 5	11 5	1225	140	250		5 8	6:8	835	1045			935	310	835
Ribbleton	626	911	1111	1231	146	256	Sats. only	514	624	841	1051	Thurs and Sats. only	SUNDAYS	941	316	841
Grimsrgh	63t	916	1116	1236	151	3 1		519	629	846	1056			946	321	846
LONGR'GE	637	922	1122	1242	157	3 7		525	635	852	11 2			952	327	852

Established 1879.

LONGRIDG	810	10 0	1140	1 5	215		320	535	655	9 0	1110		10 0	340	9 0
Grimsarg	815	10 5	1145	1 10	220	Sats. only	325	540	7 0	9 5	1115	Sats. only	10 5	345	9 5
Ribbeton	819	10 9	1149	1 14	224		329	544	7 4	9 9	......		10 9	349	9 9
Deepdale	825	1015	1155	1 26	229		335	550	710	915	1123		1015	355	915
PRESTON	832	1022	12 2	1 27	...		342	557	717	922	1130		1022	4 2	92

Garstang and Knot End Railway.

				‡	a	b		
PRESTON...dp	......	8 10	1010	1242	1242	4 30	5 26	
Garstang & Catt	......	8 30	1c31	1 1	1	4 49	5 45	
Garstang	7 0	8 40	1041	1 36	2 15	4 59	5 55	
Winmarleigh	7 10	8 55	......	1f51	2 30	5 14	6 5	
PILLING	7 25	9 10	......	2f 6	2 45	5 29	6 20	

					K		
PILLING	7 40	......	9 30	......	3 45	6 25	
Winmarleigh	7 55	......	9 45	......	4 5	3 35	
Garstang	8 5	......	9 55	1245	4 25	6 45	
Garstang & Catt	8 24	......	1013	1 26	5 14	......	
PRESTON	8 48	......	1035	1 48	5 40	..	

K Leaves Pilling at 5-45 on Sats

‡ Not on Thursdays.

† Thursdays Only.

a Sats only

b Sats excepted

The 1901 timetable of the PLR and another curio: the Garstang and Knott End Railway timetable. Courtesy: Mike Atherton Collection

PRESTON and LONGRIDGE.

Miles.	Down.		mrn	mrn	mrn	S		E	S	aft	E		S	aft	aft	aft			mrn		aft		
							Week Days.											Sundays.					
	Preston	dep.	6 9	7 5	9 10	1130	..	1210	1235	1 58	3 45	..	aft	5 19	6 44	9 22	..	..	7 5	..	5 45	..	..
1¼	Deepdale		6 5	7 10	9 16	1137	..	1215	1240	2 3	3 52	...	4 15	5 24	6 49	9 27	..	..	..	..	..	..	..
3¼	Ribbleton		..	..	9 22	1143	..	1221	1246	2 9	3 58	..	4 20	5 30	..	..	..	..	..	..	..	..	..
5	Grimsargh, for Whittingham		6 16	7 21	9 28	1149	..	1227	1252	2 15	4 4	...	4 26	5 36	7 0	9 37	..	..	7 20	..	5 59	..	..
7¼	Longridge	arr.	6 22	7 29	9 35	1156	..	1234	1259	2 22	4 11	..	4 33	5 43	7 6	9 44	..	..	7 29	..	6 6	..	..

Miles.	Up.		mrn	mrn	mrn	S		E	S	aft			S	E	aft	aft	aft		mrn		aft		
							Week Days.											Sundays.					
	Longridge	dep.	6 38	8 10	10 3	..	1230	8 1	1 15	2 40	..	4 47	5 10	6 12	7 25	9 58	..	..	7 45	..	6 25	..	..
2¼	Grimsargh, for Whittingham		6 42	8 16	10 8	..	1235	1 12	1 20	2 45	...	4 52	5 15	6 18	7 30	10 3	..	..	7 54	..	6 30	..	..
4	Ribbleton		..	8 22	1012	..	1239	1 16	1 24	2 49	..	4 56	5 19	6 22	..	..	..	..	..	..	..	..	..
5¾	Deepdale...[580, 595, 602		6 50	8 27	1017	..	1244	1 22	1 29	2 54	..	5 1	5 24	6 27	7 38	1011	..	..	..	..	..	..	..
7¼	Preston 432,437,576, arr.		6 57	8 34	1023	..	1250	1 28	1 40	3 E0	..	5 7	5 30	6 33	7 44	1017	..	..	8 11	..	6 44	..	..

E or E Except Saturdays.   S Saturdays only.

The 1929 timetable of the PLR indicated a reduction of services just one year before the withdrawal of the passenger service on 2 June 1930. Courtesy: Mike Atherton Collection

Berry Lane level crossing and signal box, Longridge. The pony, trap, and less than camera shy girls further enhance this charming Edwardian street scene. Courtesy: Longridge & District Local History Society

A group of intending passengers await the steam train at Longridge Station in 1912. Courtesy: Longridge & District Local History Society

A rare photograph of an unidentified LNWR Webb 2-4-2 tank engine entering Longridge Station. Courtesy: Longridge & District Local History Society

The LNWR 2-4-2T locomotive runs round its train, before departing for Preston. Courtesy: Longridge & District Local History Society

'Considerable interest was caused in Longridge yesterday morning when a train, totally different to the ones that have traversed the Preston to Longridge line for many years, steamed into the station. For some time the L&YR considered a means of overcoming the difficulty of the time lost in transferring the engine from one end of the train to the other at both the Preston and Longridge Stations, and a special train has been made in which the actual steam engine is situated in the centre of the train, and is controlled by the driver, who is located in the front of the first compartment. Consequently for the train to reverse the only action needed will be for the driver to change his position from one end of the train to the other. It is expected that the new trains will be on regular service within a short time'.

The experimental train, however, proved to be ephemeral and the company reverted to conventional methods of passenger operation with the Webb Class 1P 2-4-2 tank engines, later to be succeeded by the more proficient L&YR Aspinall Class 5 2-4-2T locomotives.

The popularity of the railway is mirrored by the masses of female passengers thronging Grimsargh station platform in 1909. The destination of this well-dressed group remains an enigma. The absence of crates of brown ale would tend to support a Conservative ladies' trip, or perhaps they were destined for a strait-laced religious or temperance convention. Changes in working class culture were to have a considerable effect on life styles and attitudes towards cultural activities that were to be enjoyed by railway passengers. Preston town

Longridge Station in 1914 with the 'new LNWR push and pull motor train'. A Webb 2-4-2 tank engine, between two pairs of coaches, worked the branch for a short period at this time. Courtesy: Alan Summerfield Collection

Right: The single line approach to double tracks at Longridge Station. Courtesy: Longridge & District Local History Society

Below: Grimsargh Station in 1909 was remarkably busy with intending passengers, but what was their intended destination? This classic postcard was originally posted on 22 July 1909 by Miss Jane Heyes, to her sister Eleanor in Liverpool. Courtesy: Tom Heginbotham Collection

centre seethed with activity on Saturday evenings, where cultural performances embraced a diversity of entertainment ranging from Shakespeare and opera to commercial cinema and music halls, all of which enticed passengers to the Longridge branch. Before the advent of the talkies in the 1930s resulting in Preston's burgeoning cinema industry, there were some marvellous flea pits or 'laugh and scratch,' cinemas, although these venues were not normally frequented by respectable ladies. In 1909, however, it is quite feasible that these Grimsargh passengers were lined up to echo the song, 'Let's all go to the music hall.' The years between 1905 and 1914 were the town's golden years of variety, with many great music hall performers appearing, including Marie Lloyd, who topped the bill at Preston's Royal Hippodrome on 30 October 1911. Typically, she would have engendered a good rapport with her audience by engaging in unashamed spontaneity and risqué humour. Would our ladies on the station platform have approved of this brand of humour? This will remain a mystery though, irrefutably; the local branch line had its own part to play in the promotion of an eclectic range of popular cultural activities at both ends of the branch. At Longridge there was the Palace Cinema/music hall and in the years leading up the First World War, Longridge Council rented Railway quarry from the railway company and converted it into Tootle Heights Park, at the same time providing weekend amenities including a bandstand, seats and gardens. The trains now brought railway passengers instead of mineral wagons to this particular quarry, to enjoy what proved to be a popular attraction with sightseers and visitors from Preston. Members of the brass bands played resplendent in their smart uniforms and women were dressed in Edwardian splendour with long skirts, quite often adorned by flowing pigtails.

There were dark clouds on the horizon however when Great Britain declared war on Germany on 3 August 1914. During the First World War, the railways played a vital part in the movement of troops and materials and the Longridge line was no exception. In 1915, there was a recruitment drive that used the natural amphitheatre of the quarry, for local men to join the armed forces. The Union Jack fluttered in the breeze as a series of speakers underlined Earl Kitchener's immortal plea of 'England Needs You', to supplement the British Expeditionary Force in France. The message was poignant, on 22 May 1915, when large crowds gathered at the station to watch the Longridge Brass Band play the volunteers away. [85] The First World War, of course, led to a terrible loss of life, which included many local brave soldiers who died on the battlefields of northern France, and, after the cessation of hostilities, Tootle Heights was used as the venue for a Remembrance Day service for those who had fallen. [86]

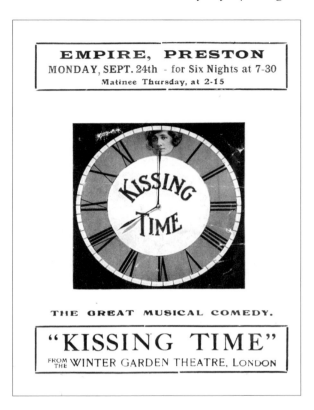

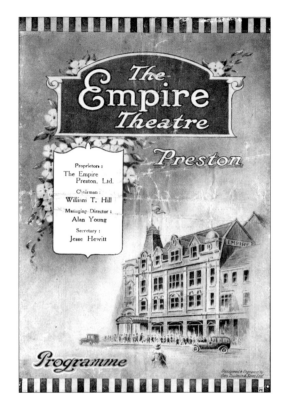

Above left: Villagers along the line were attracted to cinema and music hall performances in Preston, including 'Kissing Time', at the Preston Empire – after all, 'When all the girls are sweet, kissing time is the best time of all the times I know'. Author's Collection

Above right: Empire Theatre programme cover. Author's Collection

A Diverse Trade in Freight

Documentary evidence reveals the importance of the PLR for a diversity of freight carried by the line during the late Victorian and Edwardian eras, thus serving the interests of the wider community.

The LNWR Webb 'Cauliflower' 0-6-0 goods engines, built at Crewe in 1880, eventually succeeded the Ramsbottom DX goods engines on freight services although the latter continued to operate until the 1920s. During the first half of the twentieth century, a flexible daily mixed morning and afternoon goods train to Longridge was integrated with the prioritised passenger trains. Each shunting and trip engine had to carry a target number corresponding with the number shown in the Preston District 'Shunting Engine and Local Trip Working Book.' Shunting duties in the Longridge yard were normally undertaken by the afternoon train, which often carried heavy loads of stone back to Preston at around 6 p.m. By now the yard facilities included coal, cattle and general goods

On 13 December 1972, Sulzer Class 25 No. D5269 (25119) emerges onto the PLR from the banana warehouse on Croft's sidings. This was the last goods train to work the siding. Thereafter freight facilities were withdrawn and the siding closed. Courtesy: Peter Fitton

sidings. The stone-built goods warehouse had a through track and an internal hand-operated crane. There was also a yard crane nearby for handling heavier loads. A special livestock warehouse was built in 1918 for the Preston Farmers' Trading Society. Here, colourful freight wagons owned by different companies, complete with their own lettering embellishments on the sides, were shunted into four private sidings within the marshalling yard.

Longridge stone was transported to Preston either in the wagons of the railway company or those provided by a particular contractor, the latter qualifying for a reduction in transport charges. For example, the railway company charged about three shillings per ton to carry quarry stone and offered a discount of four pence halfpenny reduction per ton to any contractors providing their own wagons. Private wagons serving other industries worked on the same principle and typically in Longridge yard were those of the 'Wigan and Iron Company' which were light grey with black letters and those of the local firm 'Thomas Banks and Company', resplendent in black and red oxide livery with white lettering. Other traders used private wagons for distribution of their goods ranging from 'Lancashire Furnace Coke' to 'James Carter,' carrying lime from Clitheroe in peak-roofed vans. There were five more private operators working into Deepdale coal yards and occasionally some of their vehicles reached Longridge.

The commodities imported by train varied a great deal, catering for the needs of both the farming and manufacturing industries. Fertilisers, sulphite of ammonia, lime, sugar beet, cattle cake and feed were transported for use at Longridge and district farms. With certain exceptions, cattle trucks were usually integrated with the

Berry Lane, *c.* 1934, looking towards Preston, with Thomas Banks Coal Merchant in front of the signal box and Crump Oak Textile Mill right. Both the coal and textile industries provided a valuable source of freight for the branch. Courtesy: Longridge & District Local History Society

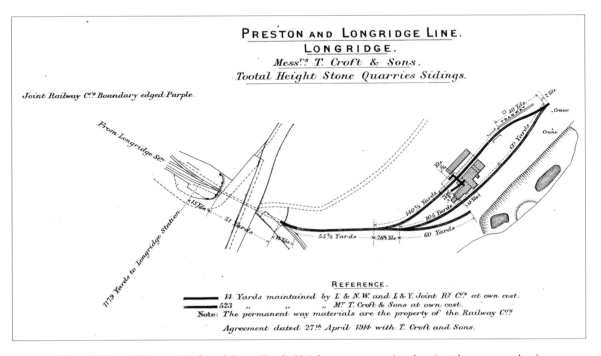

Plan of Messrs Thomas Croft and Sons, Tootle Heights stone quarries showing the quarry wharf, road tunnel and extensive sidings. Courtesy: Mike Atherton Collection

The Longridge quarry line extension looking towards Preston. In the foreground, a gradient sign of one in thirty foretells the steep climb to Tootle Heights quarries. Victoria Mill is shown on the left. Courtesy: George Whiteman Collection

The Longridge line served the wheels of industry for many years and was originally built to serve the quarrying industry. This group of men is shown in one of the Longridge quarries in 1900. Courtesy: Longridge & District Local History Society

Tootle Heights Quarry, *c.* 1905. Courtesy: Longridge & District Local History Society

In 1850, Messrs Cooper and Tullis took over Chapel Hill Quarry situated on the south side of Longridge, which was inaccessible by the railway. Horse-drawn carts transported the stone to a railway wharf at Stone Bridge sidings that was also utilised by Whittle's textile mill. This stone embankment was all that was left of the old wharf, *c.* 1966. Courtesy: Longridge & District Local History Society

goods trains, instead of forming a wholly separate train. The railway carried pigs, sheep and cattle to market and to abattoirs at Preston and Blackpool, but eventually this type of traffic declined as local farmers found it far more convenient to have their livestock picked up directly from their farms. Simultaneously, road transport started to gain the monopoly for the carriage of milk and other farming materials. Before motorised transport was established, beautiful shire horses hauling carts heavily-laden with milk churns gently trod along Long Sight Lane at Grimsargh, to link up with the trains. Milk was then carried by the railway from both Grimsargh and Longridge Stations, for onward conveyance to retail establishments in Preston.

In the immediate years leading up to the First World War, Longridge stone ceased to be the predominant form of freight transported by the railway, though Smith commented on the demise of the quarrying industry as early as 1888: 'The present state of the Longridge stone trade is not at all good. The causes of the bad trade seem to be the competition from Yorkshire and Wales, and expensive rates charged by the railway company. In this matter, and in other things, the owners of the Preston & Longridge Railway Company have displayed a poor conception of their duties as a carrying company'. [87]

Stone tonnage carried by the line was estimated to be about 250 tons per day in 1913, but by 1920 it would seem that the line's raison-d'être had faded into history. The number of workers declined between the wars, owing to competition and the increasing use of brick as a building medium. The permanent-way leading into the main quarries was finally removed in the mid 1940s, the rails being re-laid as sidings at the new Ministry of Food building which was located adjacent to the PLR at Cromwell Road, Fulwood.

The railway served the local economy by providing a vital supply route for the carriage of coal and coke to, and slag from, the foundries, mills and gas-works. Together with two iron foundries at Longridge, factories in neighbouring villages made use of the Longridge line for the transportation of heavy manufactured products and raw material, including pig iron, which was carried from west Cumberland. A foundry in the nearby village of Chipping manufactured nautical equipment, included the portholes for the doomed liner *Titanic*. These would probably have been conveyed on the PLR for onward shipping to the Harland and Wolff yards in Belfast. Several local firms specialised in the production of farm implements and others made bobbins for cotton mills all over Lancashire. Another Chipping firm, H. W. Berry, Chair-makers, also sent its finished goods to Longridge for redistribution by rail.

The textile industry remained important for the economy of Longridge and was still employing up to 30,000 people in 1911. Local historian Tom Smith recorded that manufacturers and merchants in other Lancashire towns used to point to the Longridge mills as an example of continuous work during hard times. The Stone Bridge Mill (1850-1961) was built by George Whittle and was situated alongside the railway, with its own platform to facilitate loading and unloading of materials. A short branch off the PLR led directly to the Crumpax Mill (1851-1951) situated

Right: WD 2-8-0 No. 90566 on the head-shunt at Longridge in the early 1960s; both the steam engine and Cramp Oak Mill (right) were soon to be part of Longridge's industrial past. Courtesy: George Whiteman Collection

Below: Freight timetable, 28 September 1936. Courtesy: Mike Norris

LONGRIDGE BRANCH.

WEEKDAYS.

	810	811	812	813	814	815	816	817	818	818A	819	820	821
	Engine and Brake to Preston, N.U. Yard.	Empties to Farington Jn.	Engine and Brake	Freight	Light Engine	Empties to Ince Moss.	Freight.	Freight to Preston.	Freight.	Light Engine to Preston Shed.	Engine and Brake.	Freight to Preston	Freight to Farington Jn.
Trip Number ..	25	15 MO	20 SO	20 SX	18 SO	18	19 SX	20 SO	20 SX	14 SX	19 SX	20 SX	19 SX
	a.m.	a.m.	a.m.	a.m.	a.m.	a.m.	p.m.	noon	p.m.	p.m.	p.m.	p.m.	p.m.
LONGRIDGE ....dep.	..	....	8 38	10 20			....	12 0	2 0	....	..	4 15	....
Whittle Hill.. .. .. arr.	..	....					....		2 5	....	..	..	..
Grimsargh .. .. { arr.	....	SUS- PENDED		10 30	Not after October 17th.	Is (SX) to October 17th. Inclusive.	....	12 10	....	....	..	4 25	....
{ dep.	....		..	10 45			....	12 35	....	....	..	4 33	..
Croft's Siding ....dep.	....			....			12 42	....	....	....	..	..	..
Deepdale Goods .. dep.	....	7 10		....			11 10	11 35	12 47	....	..	3 0	4 50
Deepdale Junction ♀ ..dep.	....	7 15	8*53	10*55			11 13	11 40	12*48	....	..	3 5	4*44
Maudlands.......... { arr.	..	..	8 58	11 0			11 50	..	....	....	3 10	..	5 0
{ dep.	7 15	..	..	..	Arr. Shed 11.50.		11 55	..	12 53	....	3 5	4 50	5 45
PRESTON No. 5......pass	7 21	7 26	..	..			12 0	..	12 58	....	3 8	4 52	5 55

WEEKDAYS.

	822	823	824	825	827	828	829	830	831	831A	832	833
	5.12 a.m. Freight from Preston.	Freight.	6.35 a.m. Light Engine from Preston Shed.	Freight.	Freight.	Freight.	Freight.	Freight.	Freight.	2.10 p.m. Freight from Ribble Sidings.	Freight.	8.40 p.m. Mineral from Syringe Branch.
Trip Number ..	25	18 MO	15 SO	20 SX	20 SO	20 SX	19 SX	20 SX	20 SX	14 SX	19 SX	SO
	a.m.	a.m.	a.m.	a.m.	a.m.	a.m.	a.m.		p.m.	p.m.	p.m.	p.m.
PRESTON No. 5......pass	5 18	....						Deepdale Goods depart 12.17.		2 15	..	10 50
Maudlands .. .. { arr.	5 23	5†55		7† 5	8† 5	..	11†40		....	2 20	..	10 52
{ dep.	..	6 10		7 15	8 15	9 20	11 50		12 40	..	3 53	
Deepdale Junction ♀ ..dep.	..	6 22	6 50	7*28	8*28	9 40	11*55		12*45	..	3*58	
Deepdale Goods .. arr.	....	6 27	6 52	....			12 7		....	..	4 10	
Croft's Siding							12 22					
Grimsargh .... { arr.	....			7 40	8 40				1 0	..	...	
{ dep.	....			7 50	9 0				1 15	..	..	
Whittle Hill ....dep.	....			....	....				....	2 15	....	
LONGRIDGE .... arr.	..			8 15	9 10	10 0			1 20	2 20	..	

(823: Light Engine. Works 7.10 a.m. from Deepdale. 825: Asylum Siding arrive 7.55, depart 8.5. 827: † Light Engine. 828: Arrives Deepdale 9.30 a.m. 829: † Light Engine. 833: Commences October 24th.)

in Berry Lane. Victoria Mill (1862-1935) was built and served by the railway and became the first of the Longridge mills to close. The Queen's Mill (1874-1964) was built close to the railway near to Stone Bridge Mill; however, this had no railway link and woven cloth was conveyed to the station by horse and cart. The Queen's Mill supplied curtain material for the great Cunard liner, *Queen Mary*, and, in later years, the 'Terylene' curtains for the Royal Yacht *Britannia*. It was the last of the Longridge mills to close, just before the town finally lost its rail link in 1967.

The Final Episode of Railway Mania

There was to be a final bout of railway mania that extended from the days of joint LNWR/L&YR into the LMS era. During prolonged intermittent negotiations between 1911 and 1924, the PLR was considered in further plans to link the line from Longridge Station to West Yorkshire. These plans began during April 1911, when members of the Fylde Water Board announced that the remote village of Dale Head in the Forest of Bowland was being considered as a site for the new Stocks Reservoir. In 1912, the board obtained parliamentary powers to build the reservoir, but work was delayed with the onset of the First World War. Thereafter, the principal construction work of the reservoir was carried out between 1921 and 1932.

In 1917, railway engineer Edgar Ferguson surveyed a twenty-four mile route for a single-line passenger extension of the PLR, running from Longridge to link with the Midland Railway at Hellifield. The line was planned to have stations at Chipping, Whitewell, Dunsop Bridge, Newton, Slaidburn, Tosside and Wigglesworth, passing close to the proposed Stock's Reservoir and thus befitting construction. Furthermore, the route would have traversed gradients of 1 in 75 for five miles and necessitated the installation of fifteen bridges, eight level crossings and four viaducts for the river crossings.

Ferguson estimated the costs of the line to be approximately £233,856. [88] The railway commissioners held a meeting at Slaidburn on 9 May 1918, when it was proposed to seek a light railway order. It transpired that due to a lack of funding, coupled with the Light Railway Commissioners being non-committal, the project was abandoned in 1918. Following the absorption of the LNWR into the LMS on 1 January 1923, the scheme of 1917 was again reviewed with a meeting at Clitheroe on 6 March 1923. The LMS declined to operate the railway, although they did agree to junction facilities at Longridge. The water board, appropriate local authorities and communities all supported the scheme, but declined to contribute financially. A draft order was issued on 29 November 1923, but by now enthusiasm for the line had waned considerably and the plans for the railway extension were finally cancelled in May 1924.

The Fylde Water Board had made other arrangements by the time construction work began on the reservoir in 1921. Materials used in construction work were to be conveyed by road from a rail base on the Midland Railway at Long

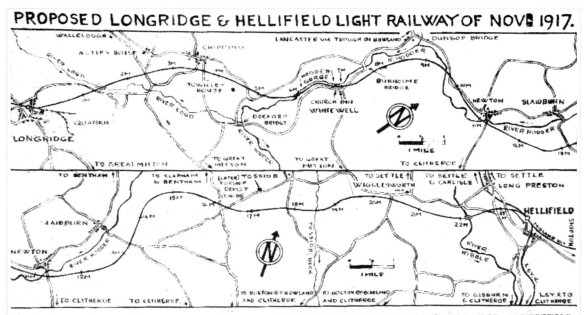

Map of the Longridge to Hellifield Light Railway. The proposed route would have passed alongside the River Hodder and between the buildings of the church and the inn at Whitewell.

Preston. Stone used in the construction of the dam was quarried locally. The quarries were linked to the construction site by a three-foot gauge railway, which also served the exchange facilities at the nearest village of Tosside; moreover, thirteen narrow gauge steam locomotives worked on site between 1921 and 1929. Today, the track bed that traversed the northern side of the reservoir, from the dam to jumble quarries at Cross of Greet, is clearly visible. Stocks reservoir was ceremoniously opened on 5 July 1932. [89]

Beginning with similar proposals seventy years earlier, this was the concluding episode of railway mania for the PLR In retrospect, none of the extravagant schemes to extend the railway into Yorkshire ever materialised and, therefore, the opportunity for the branch to have been woven into the railway network of northern England was permanently lost. On the other hand, this particular circumvention of railway mania prevented a route passing through some of Lancashire's most picturesque villages and countryside, and which, from an engineering point of view, would undoubtedly have been fraught with ongoing problems such as flooding and subsidence, especially in the Whitewell gorge.

CHAPTER EIGHT

A Lament for the Mantra, 'All stations to Longridge'

This chapter covers the years of L.M.S. ownership from 1923 until nationalisation on 1 January 1948. The LNWR was vested in the new L.M.S. as from 1 January 1923, under the North Western Midland and West Scottish Group Amalgamation Scheme 1922, dated 30 December 1922. [90] At the time of the Grouping, the L.M.S. absorbed the branch in good physical shape, despite the downward spiral of the quarrying industry.

In the years before the withdrawal of passenger services in 1930, the Company utilised several variations in motive power, culminating in the ex-L&YR Aspinall 2-4-2T superseding the less-powerful ex-LNWR Webb 2-4-2T. The L&YR engines were generally more efficient at tackling the steeply graded line than their predecessors and worked the line until the withdrawal of passenger services. At that time, locomotives usually ran chimney-first to Longridge and returned to Preston bunker/tender-first. Goods trains were hauled by ex-L&YR Barton Wright Class 2F 0-6-0 locomotives from Preston shed, including Nos. 12016, 12026, 12034, 12051, 12053.

Crucially, the introduction of local bus services in the late 1920s had a predictable outcome, with the Longridge branch achieving goods-only status only seven years after being taken over by the LMS Accordingly, the familiar scenario of the competing omnibus superseding old-fashioned trains on a local branch line bears similarities to the classic railway film, *The Titfield Thunderbolt*. The events leading up to the withdrawal of railway passenger services to Longridge were beginning to unfold even before the Grouping. As early as 18 April 1914, a report in the *Preston Guardian* said: 'Good Friday saw many visitors to Jeffrey Hill and Tootle Heights which have become popular picnic spots. The bus service between Preston and Longridge was exceptionally busy'.

The new bus companies serving the principal stations were encouraged to be in direct competition with the railway. For example, in May 1927, the motion was carried by Grimsargh Parish Council: 'That the Preston Town Clerk should be asked to provide equal facilities for the buses serving Grimsargh and Longridge

Regular motive power for many years on Longridge freight turns was the ex-L&YR Aspinall 3F 0-6-0. These two examples, Nos. 52271 (left) and 52140, were photographed at Manchester Victoria on 2 April 1960. Courtesy: Peter Fitton

An equally common type on the passenger workings was the ex-L&YR Aspinall 2P 2-4-2T. No. 50781, photographed at Southport Chapel Street on 31 August 1959. This particular locomotive was actually used on the line when based at Lostock Hall shed in 1951. Courtesy: Peter Fitton

which are given to others'. Hence, by the late 1920s, buses operated by the Pilot, Majestic and Claremont companies that emanated from Clitheroe and Preston, were on track to eclipse the PLR passenger service.

Quite apart from the gradual increase of motor traffic and rival bus services, there was also social and economic gloom caused by a world trade recession, following the Wall Street Crash. As the depression deepened between 1929 and 1933, thousands of workers became unemployed. The combined foregoing factors, coupled with a rationalisation policy by the LMS, contributed to the line being scheduled to close on Monday, 2 June 1930. What the railways did to earlier forms of transport such as the stagecoach and canal transport was now beginning to happen to the rural branch line. In the absence of a Sunday service, the last train from Longridge was the 9.58 p.m. on Saturday, 31 May 1930. It was hauled by ex-L&YR Aspinall, Class 5 2-4-2T No. 10646, which had been a regular engine on the branch. As always, there was more than a tinge of sadness at the time of closure and a column in the *Lancashire Daily Post* on Monday, 2 June 1930, evoked those feelings: 'It was as well that someone should have remembered, for there was nothing at Preston to indicate that engine 10646 was to make the last passenger journey on the 90-years-old line. But at the village stations it was different, for it was their train and they were seeing it for the last time. When the train steamed out seven minutes late, it suffered the indignity of having to pull up within a few hundred yards of the platform, to give way to main line trains. Perhaps after all there was recognition of the mournful last trip, as the unlit carriages ran through gloomy yards and into dark tunnels.

'After leaving town, the 9.22pm came into its own at Longridge. The train's arrival was heralded by three short reports, caused by fog detonators placed on the line. The cobble stone platform was crowded and the booking clerk was issuing the last tickets. "No, I won't book return", said someone. Unusual interest was taken in the coupling of the engine for the last time. An optimist with a pocket camera tried to immortalise the event and a Clergyman, to give it a Benediction, as it were, shook hands with the driver and fireman. A porter gave the all clear by whistling with his fingers and on the stroke of ten, the Longridge to Preston train started for the last time.

'Passengers leaned out to wave to those left on the station, the engine whistled a prolonged goodbye to the village and the bridges and embankments were lined with people, anxious to see the last train. Then came a stretch of line studded with fog signals. Report after report rang out, and, as the train approached each station, the steam whistle sounded and more fog signals exploded. There were groups of officials at each of the stations and passengers and onlookers insisted on shaking hands with the driver. There were at least 40 detonations before the train emerged from Deepdale tunnels. At Maudland there was an enforced delay and the train stopped over the shadowed canal. Reaching Preston station exactly an hour after leaving for the outward journey, the driver and fireman and a few

Ex-L&YR Aspinall 2-4-2 tank, number 10646 is shown at Grimsargh Station on 31 May 1930, while working the last official passenger train. Driver Billington, of Lostock Hall Shed, bids a fond farewell to stationmaster Harold Lathom. Author's Collection

Grimsargh level crossing and the British Railways Station photographed on 22 August 1964, by which time a firm of builder's merchants were using it, although the original station notice-board advertises the fact that 'Parcels and goods traffic is dealt with at this station – enquire within.' Meanwhile, WD 'Austerity' Class 8F 2-8-0 No. 90675 lets off steam in the goods yard. Courtesy: Alan Castle

passengers inspected a wreath, which had been tied onto the engine on the return journey. A few minutes afterwards the train ran into the sheds and so ended the service which was begun with the hope of linking Lancashire with Yorkshire on 1st May 1840'.

At Grimsargh Station, the crew of the last train bid a fond farewell to the proud stationmaster Harold Lathom, who continued to serve the local community as churchwarden and organist at Grimsargh St Michael's Church. Driver Billington of Lostock Hall shed summed up the effect on local communities such as Grimsargh, in describing the last journey, 'Use is second nature and people get to know each other, that is why they are sorry'.

The closure event was not without precedent in rural Lancashire, for a new form of transport had superseded local branch lines and they were no longer wanted. Other local passenger branches closing in 1930 included the five-mile long Lancaster to Glasson Dock line and the Garstang, Pilling and Knott End railway.

However, this was not quite the end of the line for passengers on the PLR, because following the cessation of regular passenger services on 2 June 1930, several passenger excursions ran from Longridge throughout the 1930s. An annual event to look forward to by the Oddfellows' Society was a trip to the seaside from Longridge and Grimsargh Stations. A special passenger train was diagrammed to run via the East Lancashire line and Preston Junction to Blackpool. Annual excursions organised by the Church of England Sunday Schools ran from Longridge to Southport between 1925 until at least 1936. Also excursions organised by Lancashire County Education Committee for local day schools ran from Longridge to destinations which included Liverpool, Edinburgh, London and Stratford. [91] Miss Olive Simm, who resided in one of the cottages at Red Scar and who was a former pupil at St Michael's School, Grimsargh, recalled a school rail trip from the disused Grimsargh Station on 22 May 1936. A search of the Grimsargh School log revealed the appropriate entry recorded for posterity: 'The School was closed today to allow fourteen children and two teachers to visit Worcester and Stratford on Avon, on an excursion organised by the LMS Railway Company'.

The WHR and PLR feature in the history of two world wars. During the First World War, wounded soldiers were treated at Whittingham Hospital. With the outbreak of the Second World War, the rural villages of Grimsargh and Goosnargh played a part in the evacuation of hundreds of thousands of urban children to the countryside of Britain. A special main line train hauling many carriages steamed into the closed LMS Grimsargh Station only two weeks after the outbreak of war. The evacuees from the Manchester area had labels on their collars with their names on so that brothers and sisters would not be separated. The children were processed at the Grimsargh Assembly Hall and provided with local accommodation. Because of overcrowding at Grimsargh St Michael's School, a letter had been sent to the Hospital Management, requesting that the

Whittingham trains be used to link with future diagrams arriving at Grimsargh, in order to convey the overspill of evacuees to the village school at Goosnargh. However, the unfortunate children were deemed one group that were to be excluded from the Whittingham trains, on the grounds that 'it is inadvisable that the hospital railway be use as a means of conveyance for these children.'

During the Second World War, the local Home Guard, led by a certain Colonel Potter, marched into the Grimsargh stationmaster's office and agonised over his strategy to keep the Fuhrer firmly on the German rail network. In particular, this erstwhile leader of men focussed on keeping a ceaseless watch out for German paratroopers and establishing the identity of any suspicious individuals. This was especially so for those suspiciously loitering near Courtaulds' Factory, local bridges and the new LMS sidings serving Ministry of Supply refrigerated depots built for the storage of emergency rations at Ribbleton and Grimsargh. The Home Guard valiantly met their overall challenges, clandestine operations taking place within the hallowed walls of Grimsargh Station and the nearby Plough Inn being entrusted to the venerable soldiers. We will never know their official secrets, although ultimately not even Dad's Army could have saved the branch from closure.

Freight Services (1930–1948)

After the withdrawal of the PLR passenger service, both Grimsargh and Longridge Stations remained open for parcels and goods traffic until closure of the eastern section of the branch in November 1967. The freight timetable for 28 September 1936 illustrates a morning and afternoon goods train working through to Longridge, with additional trains working as far as Deepdale goods yard and Croft's siding. Ex-L&YR Aspinall Class 3F 0-6-0 and ex-LNWR (Super D) Class 7F 0-8-0 goods locomotives were regularly seen on the branch during the years of both LMS and British Railways ownership. These latter two classes continued to work the goods trains until the 1950s.
Typical products carried by the railway included timber, new bottles for dairies, sugar beet for farmers and coal for industrial and domestic consumption.

Before the war and during the immediate post-war years, Robert and James Wilkinson conducted a business as coal merchants, delivering coal from the sidings situated behind Grimsargh Station. After the coal wagons were shunted into the goods sidings, the burly brothers transferred it to their own classic commercial vehicles for local delivery. Nothing was too much trouble when the telephone rang and the caller informed them that 'I have run out of coal'. They would go down to the yard and load up two or three bags onto a 3-ton Morris lorry, which was purchased new in 1933. Like its drivers, this vehicle was no stranger to hard work for, during thirty years of active service, it covered over half a million miles, carrying over 40,000 tons of coal.

With the demise of Preston shed, this class of loco – once so common on the Longridge branch – had all but disappeared from the Preston area. Surviving No. 49451 was specially loaned to Lostock Hall shed from Wigan (Springs Branch) to work a special tour of north-west branch lines including the PLR. Courtesy: Martin Willacy

Ex-L&YR Aspinall 0-6-0 3F No. 52182 about to leave Longridge Station with a short train for Preston in the 1950s. Courtesy: M. Kerfoot

Ex-LYR Aspinall class 3F 0-6-0 No. 52336 crosses over a water installation near Dam House Farm, Grimsargh, *c.* 1952. George Whiteman Collection

The Wilkinson Brothers were a firm of coal merchants based in Grimsargh station yard. They were frequently called out to load heavy bags onto one of three classic vehicles. Courtesy: David Wilkinson

Above: The large deliveries of coal and raw materials for Courtaulds' Factory justified the acquisition of two industrial Peckett 0-4-0-saddle tank locomotives. The proud crew are seen alongside the brand new Courtaulds No. 1 engine *c.* 1938. Courtesy: Ian Grayston

Left: A one mile branch from the Exchange Sidings on the PLR led to extensive sidings within the factory. Courtesy: Ian Grayston

Peckett No. 2 'Miranda,' photographed on a winter's day in February 1967, in front of Fred Dibnah's famous twin biros Courtaulds' chimneys. David Hindle

Between turns of duty, 'Miranda' emerges from the engine-shed at Courtaulds' Red Scar Works in February 1967. David Hindle

Stanier Class 8F 2-8-0 48764 and Peckett No. 1, 'Caliban', at Courtaulds' Exchange Sidings in the early 1960s. Courtesy: Alan Middleton

The local agricultural scene at Grimsargh and Longridge meant that, occasionally, the railway carried livestock traffic for the domestic meat trade. There were a few bizarre workings, however, that caused local residents to stand and stare in amazement. The first such working took place in 1935, when Miss Nellie Carbis, the headmistress of the small village school of St Michael's, Grimsargh, and her pupils, witnessed the extraordinary sight of a train they dubbed 'Noah's Ark.' From the classroom window, the village schoolchildren had a good view of a special train organised by the Bradley family of Preesall, which was transporting their entire farm stock to Grimsargh Station. At the station, the cattle were rounded-up in the pens at the end of the platform, before proceeding through Grimsargh to their ultimate destination at Boot Farm, Alston, and pastures new.

In January 1936, it was reported in the *Lancashire Evening Post* that Mrs Kate Hollas, the last tenant of Red Scar, Grimsargh, was moving to a farm near Swindon. Consequently, a special train had been ordered to run from Longridge to Wiltshire, to transport the entire farm stock and animals. The *Lancashire Evening Post* reported that: 'Resembling a "Noah's Ark", a train left Longridge this afternoon for Highworth, near Swindon, a distance of two hundred miles. It comprised eleven trucks of livestock, thirteen of farm implements and sectional cabins; practically the whole of the farm stock from Holworth and Hacking

Hobbs Farms at Longridge, the property of Mrs Kate Hollas of "Red Scar", Grimsargh. Mrs Hollas has taken up Parsonage Farm, Highworth, following the sale of Red Scar, to Messrs Courtaulds' rayon factory. There were on the train six shires, a hunter and two foals, a Shetland pony, forty-five sheep, a bull, fifteen cows, twenty seven stirks, eighteen yearlings and four calves. The farm implements included carts, traps, plough, harrow, turnip-cutter, harness and feeding utensils. The cows were milked before leaving and will be at "Parsonage Farm," in time for the early morning milking. By 9am tomorrow it is expected that the whole of the livestock will have been safely transported and will be grazing in the fields of Wiltshire'.

A 'knight in shining armour' proved a real saviour for freight services on the PLR during 1938, when Messrs. Courtaulds opened a huge factory at Ribbleton, five miles to the north-east of Preston. It became one of the largest viscose works in Britain and was linked to exchange sidings on the PLR by a one mile private single-line, which was worked by two Peckett 0-4-0-saddle tanks and, from 1967, by a Sentinel diesel, until closure of the factory in 1980. Domestic and industrial coal, always an important commodity carried by the railway, became the mainstay of freight operations, with several flexible coal trains a day serving the sidings at Deepdale and Courtaulds for industrial and home consumption.

CHAPTER NINE

Towards the ultimate buffer stops

The period under review covers the events leading up to the ultimate closure of the last segment of the branch and the current terminal decay of the abandoned tracks. During the second half of the twentieth century, there were three sequential closure phases affecting the PLR The first freight cutback was from Longridge to Courtaulds factory in 1967. The next section to close was from Courtaulds to Deepdale junction in 1980, culminating in the closure of the final stretch of track between Maudland Junction and the coal distribution depot in Fletcher Road, Deepdale, in 1994.

The LMS ceased to exist on 1 January 1948, when British Railways was nationalised. After the war, the story of the branch continued with a downward spiral of freight services. Between 1948 and 1967, the closure of all four of the Longridge cotton mills was to have an adverse effect on the coal and general freight traffic. A further decline in coal traffic came with the closure of the Whittingham Hospital branch in 1957. The gradual transfer of allegiance from rail to road transport augured badly for the branch, with a reduction of the freight service beyond Courtaulds' Sidings to Grimsargh and Longridge. The morning and afternoon Longridge goods trains were reduced to a single morning train by the 1950s. During the same era, the branch had up to four freight trains per day working to Courtaulds' Exchange Sidings, Monday to Friday and two on Saturdays. Only the second morning train worked through to the Longridge terminus.

The monotony of the scheduled freight service was briefly alleviated by several brief and memorable events. For example, the post-war building of large suburban housing estates at Ribbleton saw the branch playing a crucial part in the installation of electricity supplies. British Railways gave permission for the electricity authority to lay their cables beside the line. I witnessed this unusual operation from Crowell Road Bridge, on a bitterly cold Sunday in January 1955. The normal method of one engine in steam over the single-track to Grimsargh and Longridge was suspended on a day when the line was to see no other traffic. The special train had a couple of the familiar ex-LNWR 7F 0-8-0 locomotives,

Nos. 49150 and 49382, at either end, and between the old locomotives were several cable wagons and a steam breakdown crane, which was depositing cable drums at the side of the track. The engine at the head of the train shunted empty wagons into the sidings outside the Ministry of Food cold storage depot.

Special Passenger Workings

Opportunistic passengers enjoyed organised rail-tours run by locomotive societies during the last two decades of the line. The Stephenson Locomotive Society/ Manchester Locomotive Society ran their 'North Lancashire Railtour' along the PLR on 1 May 1954. For an inclusive price of 80 shillings there was an opportunity to travel behind a Fowler, Class 4MT 2-6-4 tank locomotive No. 42316, from Preston to Longridge and return. The train then slowly negotiated several more branch lines, including Garstang-Pilling, Lancaster-Glasson Dock and Arnside-Hincaster Junction. Speed was not to exceed 15 miles per hour between Gastang and Catterall and Pilling in each direction and it was pointed out that 'Pilling platform is in a bad state of repair. Care must be taken on alighting there'.

The line to Pilling served the farming industry and was the last segment of the former branch to Knott End to close.

The joint Stephenson Locomotive Society and Manchester Locomotive Society rail tour of 1 May 1954 arrives at Longridge Station, running bunker-first, behind Crewe North depot's Fowler Class 4MT 2-6-4T No. 42316. Courtesy: Gordon Biddle

The SLS/MLS tour of 1 May 1954 at Longridge Station. The train was about to set off at 2.15 p.m., hauled by No. 42316, for a tour of yet more long-closed passenger lines in north Lancashire and Cumbria. Courtesy: R. H. Hughes – Manchester Locomotive Society

No. 42316 runs round its train at Garstang. Meanwhile, the identity of the young onlooker may yet be revealed! Courtesy: R. H. Hughes – Manchester Locomotive Society

W699 BRITISH RAILWAYS (M)
DAY EXCURSION
The Stephenson Locomotive Society
& Manchester Locomotive Society

1st MAY, 1954
NORTH LANCS RAIL TOUR
PRESTON TO

(2001)

SANDSIDE & BACK
via Longridge, Lostock Hall, Pilling,
Glasson Dock, Arnside, Oxenholme,
Lancaster Old

THIRD CLASS
FOR CONDITIONS SEE OVER

0063   0063

A special day excursion ticket was issued for the 'North Lancashire Rail tour' which embraced the Longridge branch line. Courtesy: Mike Atherton

Ex-LNWR Class 7F 0-8-0 No. 49451 approaching the occupation bridge near Grimsargh, with the 'Mid Lancashire Rail tour,' heading for Longridge on 22 September 1962. Courtesy: Peter Fitton

Ex-LNWR class 7F 0-8-0 No. 49451 near St Michael's Church, Grimsargh, with the RCTS 'Mid Lancs Rail tour,' heading for Longridge on 22 September 1962. Courtesy: Peter Fitton

With Victoria Mill in the background, 'Super D' No. 49451 prepares to haul its train tender-first from Longridge back to Preston with what would ultimately prove to be the very last steam-hauled passenger train to work the branch. Courtesy: Peter Fitton

Special arrangements were made for passengers desirous of travelling on the WHR and an extract from the joining instructions read as follows: 'The visit to the Whittingham railway has been made possible through the kindness of the hospital authorities, and M. T. Smith, group engineer. Special transport to Grimsargh has been arranged. Buses leave the forecourt of Preston station 11.30am and 12.30pm ... A small charge of approximately two shillings will be made to cover the cost of transport and expenses on the Whittingham line. The promoting societies wish to take this opportunity of placing on record their sincere appreciation of the hospital authority's action in placing their line at our disposal for two hours. Parties will also be conducted over other engineering installations on the site'.

The very last passenger train of all to traverse the entire length of the PLR, departed from Longridge at 2.27 p.m. on Saturday, 22 September 1962. This was the Railway Correspondence & Travel Society's 'Mid-Lancs Rail-Tour' and the adventurous itinerary was available for an inclusive fare of £1 6s. Appropriately, an ex-LNWR Class 7F 0-8-0 No. 49451, provided the motive power for the five-coach train of former LMS stock, this comprising three corridor coaches, a half brake and a buffet car, at the same time graphically placing on record a new form of railway mania being generated in the 1960s. Indeed, two of the three locomotives (including No. 49451) to be used on various stages of the tour that day had previously been specially cleaned for the occasion by a small group of intending passengers!

Not surprisingly, this was not the last passenger excursion on the truncated branch; such a melancholy distinction being given to a three-car diesel multiple unit, organised by the Branch Line Society, that went as far as Courtaulds' Exchange Sidings and returned via Deepdale Goods yard on a particularly wet autumn day on 25 October 1969. The PLR featured in an itinerary embracing other interesting closed passenger lines in Lancashire and Cumbria. [92]

Stanier 8F 2-8-0 No. 48002 reverses from the station yard onto the main line at Grimsargh, while working a special tour organised by the North West Branch of the LCGB on 1 April 1966. Long before the days of health and safety constraints, a more liberal outlook permitted the members to be conveyed in three brake vans that were attached to the regular daily freight train – happy days! Courtesy: Alan Castle

'Steam in the landscape' Stanier Class 5 No. 45110 in pleasant countryside between Grimsargh and Ribbleton. Courtesy: Alan Middleton

Running tender-first, Stanier 8F 2-8-0 No. 48002 passes the old cattle pen on Grimsargh platform with three brake vans and heads towards Preston. Courtesy: Alan Castle

The unauthorised tampering with the brake mechanism on coal trucks at the exchange sidings led to a derailment on the Courtaulds' siding in 1965. Brush type 4 diesel (Class 47) with the breakdown train at Courtaulds' Exchange Sidings in 1965. Courtesy: Alan Middleton

With Courtaulds' factory in the background, the breakdown crane from the motive power depot at Lostock Hall recovers the coal trucks following a derailment in 1965. Courtesy: Ian Grayston

Swan-song for Steam to Longridge

During the last two decades of steam, the branch drew on an assortment of regular locomotives, including Ivatt Class 2MT 2-6-0 Nos. 46429/30, which came new to the Preston shed *c.* 1950. These two were replaced around 1956 by new and almost identical Standard Class 2MT 2-6-0s Nos. 78036/37. Until their demise or transfer away in 1960, the ex-LNWR Class 7F 0-8-0s from Preston shed often worked the morning service, while ex-L&YR Aspinall Class 3F 0-6-0s from Lostock Hall depot usually operated the afternoon diagram.

The 1960s brought an interesting mixture of locomotives to the branch, these including Stanier Class 8F 2-8-0s, 5MT 4-6-0s and 2-6-0s, 'Crab' 2-6-0s and WD 8F 2-8-0s. In their twilight years, Class 6P5F 'Jubilee' 4-6-0 express passenger locomotives also suffered the indignity of hauling a few trucks to Longridge and appeared almost weekly. The last scheduled steam-worked goods train of all to Longridge was hauled by Lostock Hall shed's Ivatt Class 4MT 2-6-0 No. 43027. This final visit occurred some time after the daily trip working had gone over to regular diesel working and, although the exact date is uncertain, it would have occurred at some time in the autumn of 1967.

Dieselisation brought English Electric Class 40s, Sulzer Class 25s and, latterly, occasional Class 45s, along with Class 08 350hp diesel shunters, which were engaged on shorter trains.

Riddles Standard Class 2MT 2-6-0 No. 78036 takes precautions while coming off the P.L.R. at Maudland on 24 March 1962. Courtesy: Chris Spring

Stanier Class Five 4-6-0 No. 45110 at Courtaulds in 1968. This locomotive was given a reprieve from a humiliating fate by ultimately being secured for preservation on the Severn Valley Railway. David Hindle

Stanier Class 5MT 4-6-0 No. 45055 makes a splendid sight as it passes the Ribbleton housing estates on 31 July 1968. Courtesy: Chris Spring

With the Courtaulds' branch in the foreground, Stanier Class Five 4-6-0 No. 45110 ambles along the branch towards the Exchange Sidings. Courtesy: Alan Middleton

An unidentified Standard Class '4MT' 4-6-0 passes the cattle pen at Grimsargh Station while *en route* to Preston in 1967. Courtesy: George Whiteman Collection

A view from the footplate at Longridge Station as WD 'Austerity' Class 2-8-0 No. 90675 commences its return journey to Preston on 22 August 1964. Courtesy: Alan Castle

Doctor Beeching's Prescription

Sadly, by 1962 there were dark clouds on the horizon for the future of the branch. A certain Doctor Beeching had heard about the Longridge line and so had the general manager at Euston. The Doctor had already issued an immediate prescription, which referred to an unprecedented contraction of the national railway network, but was euphemistically described in an official document as *The Reshaping of British Railways*. Correspondence, dated 16 March 1966 and addressed to the hierarchy of Preston railway management, was given the same ominous heading, when they were reminded: 'The Longridge Branch is 6 miles 76 chains long. The single-line branches off the main Preston to Lancaster line in a north-easterly direction and is used for freight service only. It is proposed to close the branch between Courtaulds' Sidings and Longridge, a distance of 3 miles 48 chains, and to close the Longridge and Grimsargh freight facilities and remove all assets'. The general manager at Euston endorsed the closure of the line from Courtaulds to Longridge with a harsh and succinct communication: 'It will be severed at 3 miles 69 chains, making the route closure 3 miles 19 chains. The line will close on 6th November, 1967'. [93]

Poignantly, 127 years of railway history were written-off on Friday, 3 November 1967, when an unidentified diesel-shunter hauled the final official diagrammed goods train from Longridge to Preston. Local farmer Peter Wild, of Dixon's Farm, filmed the diesel engine and guard's van working light from Grimsargh to Longridge to collect some trucks and captured the unceremonious event on celluloid. On the return journey, it is seen shunting and collecting about ten more trucks at Grimsargh sidings. Finally, the teachers and children of Grimsargh St Michael's School are shown waving goodbye to the train, while exhibiting a board bearing the words, 'Last train on the Longridge line, 3rd November 1967'. The official closure date of the line between Courtaulds' No. 2 Ground Frame and Longridge was Monday 6 November 1967 with no trains scheduled to run over the weekend.

However, there was to be a momentary stay of execution when a Class 08 diesel again crossed over the abandoned tracks, with a single truck containing cinders to upgrade a footpath at Longridge on 5 March 1968. Then that really was the end for trains to Longridge and, by July 1968, the track had been lifted. A further dispatch was issued by the signal and telegraph department informing engine crews that the execution had been carried out: 'The single-line from Deepdale Junction Signal Box has been severed, from a point 350 yards on the Longridge side of Courtaulds' No. 2 Ground Frame'.[94]

An unidentified 350hp Class 08 0-6-0 diesel at Courtaulds. Courtesy: Alan Middleton

At the sharp end of operations driver and fireman take control of their locomotive. Courtesy: Alan Middleton

On the day of the final goods train from Longridge on 3 November, 1967, Grimsargh level crossing gates were opened for the last time to permit an old rival, the Longridge bus, to upstage the railway – this time for ever. Courtesy: Eileen Parker

How Grimsargh Station looked at the time of the visit by H. C. Casserley on 26 April 1951.
Courtesy: HCC/RMC

An unidentified Stanier Class 5MT 2-6-0 at Grimsargh with a light goods train from Longridge.
Courtesy: George Whiteman Collection

This wintertime photograph of the centre of Grimsargh depicts the permanently closed crossing gates and station prior to demolition. Courtesy: Eileen Parker

The demolition gangs soon moved in to successfully obliterate 127 years of fascinating history from the landscape. They are seen here at Grimsargh Station. Courtesy: George Whiteman Collection

The Final Curtain: Diesels Replace Steam on the Segmented PLR

Following closure of the line between Courtaulds and Longridge the reduced Longridge line sustained only one weekday coal train that latterly ran tender-first to Courtaulds' factory with about twenty wagons. By now, both diesel and steam locomotives were working this section, with steam seeing regular service up to the official end of steam traction in August 1968.

Thereafter, diesel locomotives held the monopoly at the sharp end of trains to Courtaulds for another twelve years, when market forces brought-about closure of the factory in 1980 with nearly 3,000 people being made redundant. Accordingly, the second major section of the line to close was a substantial section of track from a point 500 yards east of Deepdale Junction, through Ribbleton to Courtaulds' Exchange Sidings. A Class 40 locomotive ran to Courtaulds on Friday 8 February 1980, with a final consignment of coal for the factory, and which was carried in twenty sixteen-ton hopper wagons. The return trip with the empties took place four days later and was worked by Sulzer Class 25 No. 25.142. For over forty years, Courtaulds' Preston factory was one of the largest viscose works in Britain, and its demise signalled the end of the two 385 ft high Courtaulds' chimneys, which were referred to by the late Fred Dibnah as 'The Two Preston Biros'.

Nevertheless, it was not quite the end of the beleaguered PLR Following the closure of Courtaulds, a short section of the double-track route survived until 1994. This truncated section ran from Maudland through the tunnel to Deepdale Junction and thence over the original route of the PLR to the coal concentration distribution depot at Fletcher Road, Deepdale, and the site of the original Deepdale Street Station. The depot had been given fresh impetus in 1969, when Preston became the British Rail coal distribution depot for central Lancashire. Improvements included hoppers and loading facilities to service around five trains a day, which gradually dwindled to about three trains a week by the early 1990s.

Martin Hilbert photographed a Class 37 diesel No. 37.706, hauling twenty coal hoppers to Deepdale Sidings on 27 August 1993, but then gradually without ceremony the historic PLR faded completely off the railway network in 1994, when British Coal ceased operations at the Deepdale depot. Under the mass Railtrack transfers of land scheme, an agreement was made for a land sale in February 1996, followed by a Deed of Covenant with Preston County Borough Council on 31 March 1998. [95] The implementation of this measure saw the Deepdale Sidings removed.

There is a strong possibility that the railway itself might be reincarnated as a modern tramway for the expanding City of Preston, for, on 22 August 2008, it was reported that: 'City leaders are in talks on bringing a light railway network to Preston. The vision is to have tram-like vehicles running on disused rail lines through Deepdale, Brookfield and Red Scar'. [96] At the time of writing the old line is being adapted as a test tramway at Ribbleton and the first tram has been delivered for trials along a section of the Longridge branch at Deepdale, but only time will tell if such an ambitious plan will reach fruition.

A Portfolio of Steam and Diesel Locomotives

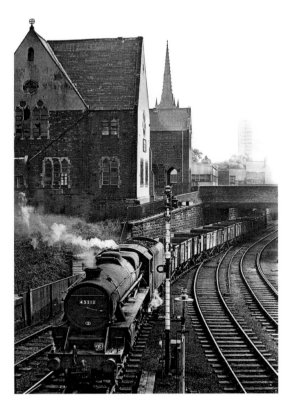

Left: Stanier 4-6-0 No. 45212 shunting alongside the site of the demolished Maudland Curve Signal Box. This location is the site of the former Maudland Bridge Station, closed in 1885, and access to which was afforded by means of Cold Bath Street Bridge in the background. Courtesy: Alan Castle

Below: On a winter's day in 1966, Stanier 2-8-0 No. 48679 passes the remains of Deepdale Station with 'No. 63 Target', a designated daily working between Farington Junction and Deepdale Coal Sidings. Courtesy: Alan Castle

Stanier 2-8-0 48679 shunting coal wagons at Deepdale Sidings. Courtesy: Alan Castle

WD 'Austerity' Class 8F 2-8-0 No. 90675 shunting at Courtaulds' Exchange Sidings on 22 August 1964. Courtesy: Alan Castle

The end of steam at Courtaulds came in 1967, when the two Pecketts were replaced by a Sentinel diesel-shunter. It is seen here adjacent to the coal fired boiler house on 9 February 1980. Courtesy: Martin Hilbert

In 1968, Peckett No. 1 'Caliban' was hauled by a Sulzer Class 25 diesel No. 5286 from Courtaulds' Sidings (here depicted) to 'Steamtown, Carnforth' before later seeking pastures new on the Lakeside & Haverthwaite Railway. Courtesy: David Eaves

Commensurate with the closure of Courtaulds' Factory, the very last train to negotiate the exchange sidings and to traverse the remaining three miles of the former Preston to Longridge railway through Ribbleton was Class 25 No. 25.142 in February 1980. Courtesy: Martin Hilbert

Courtaulds Sentinel diesel shunter pauses under Longridge Road Bridge on the one mile branch. Courtesy: Martin Hilbert

An atypical scenario for the Longridge line in 1978! A Class 25 diesel passes the site of Deepdale Station, *en route* to Deepdale Junction with an unusual train of mixed wagons, instead of the customary coal train. Courtesy: Martin Hilbert

On 9 May 1980, English Electric Class 40 No. 40.109 disgraces itself by running off the track on trap points near Deepdale. The Springs Branch Breakdown Train is in attendance. Courtesy: Mick Langton

Having propelled empty trucks out of Deepdale yard, blue-liveried Class 37 No. 37.244 waits at
Deepdale Junction, bound for Washwood Heath on 3 May 1990. The locomotive is standing on the
line built in 1850; the original PLR line built in 1840 is to the right. Courtesy: Martin Hilbert

Cardiff Canton's Class 37 No. 37.222, in Railfreight Coal Sector livery, waits to enter Deepdale
Coal Distribution Centre, with a train of coal hoppers, on 25 July 1991. It is near the site of the
first Deepdale Station. Courtesy: Martin Hilbert

Portland Street Bridge was an ideal location for photography, as this photo of Class 20s No. 20.056 and 20.072, heading towards Deepdale Junction, clearly illustrates. Courtesy: Martin Hilbert

An Unforgiving Landscape

Today there is nowhere to hide the 1960s effects of the Beeching legacy and consequently a few disused stations, bridges, tell-tale signs of earthworks and visible scars are all that remain in an unforgiving landscape as a phantom of a railway. At Maudland one remaining track was still discernible in 2010, disappearing into ever-thickening undergrowth towards Skeffington Road. There is little evidence of the main level crossings and the goods sidings at Deepdale yard have become transformed into retail outlets and offices. A substantial length of the track between Ribbleton and Grimsargh is now a footpath/cycle track. Ribbleton Station still stands, although the adjacent stone bridge that once carried Gamull Lane was demolished to facilitate a road-widening scheme soon after closure of the line to Courtaulds in 1980. The bridge over the M6 motorway (the former Preston Bypass – Britain's first motorway – opened in December 1958) has also now been removed. At Grimsargh, the narrow over-bridge survives as a relic of the line. East of Grimsargh, most of the old track-bed has been reclaimed for agricultural use or for housing development. At Longridge Stone Bridge, a blue heritage plaque briefly describes the history of the line.

Tootle Heights quarries have again reverted to a site of recreation as a caravan park. The original tunnel to the quarry and the base of a quarry crane survive as important isolated remnants of the upper line, a fact which was duly recognised by Ribble Valley Council who undertook external restoration work of the site in 2002 with the placing of an interpretation board detailing the history of the line on what is now John Smith Park. There is little evidence of the trading wharf that once extended for approximately 32 yards towards the tunnel.

Mercifully in 2010, passengers at the remarkably intact Longridge Station of 1872 have given way to a combined 'Old Station,' café, business and heritage centre thanks to a substantial grant from the heritage lottery fund. Not quite full circle, though perhaps a sizzling hot water geyser and Rachmaninov's music might stimulate a possible romantic 'brief encounter,' Longridge style, especially if one has a good imagination. 'Hello, how lovely to meet you, do you come here often, how about a date? There is a good film on this week at the Longridge Palace, they even have double seats for courting couples.' – 'Err thanks but no thanks!'

The new look Longridge 'Old Station' heritage centre in 2010.

Before entering Maudland tunnel, the branch originally passed over the Lancaster Canal, where Maudland Bridge Station was once situated. The girder bridge (foreground) marks the course of the canal between Preston and Kendal and the original terminus of the line. Courtesy: David Eaves

At Maudland, the track passed through a deep-walled cutting supported by wooden beams and under-bridges at Cold Bath Street, Pollard Street and Radnor Street. The western portal of the Maudland Tunnel, depicted here, survives as a relic to the work consignment undertaken in building the FP&WRR extension in 1850. Courtesy: Ian Race

At Blackpool Road, Ribbleton, rosebay willow herb provides a suitable foreground for the double track-bed that was conceived in connection with the proposals of 1846 by the FP&WRR to extend the line into West Yorkshire. Courtesy: David Eaves

By 17 April 1974, the tracks have long been lifted and Grimsargh Station awaits its fate. Courtesy: Alan Summerfield

At Grimsargh, along a prominent embankment ran the Preston to Longridge branch line. On a summer's day, with the fells of Bowland in the background, 'Billy' pauses alongside all that is left of the track bed and a forlorn gradient sign. David Hindle

The bridge over the M6 Motorway (the former Preston Bypass – Britain's first motorway) has now been removed so if the tramway proposal goes ahead a new crossing of the motorway will have to be considered. Courtesy: David Eaves.

The remains of the track-bed that formerly led to Lord's Quarry, on the bottom line. David Hindle

The Langden Fold development was built on the site of the WHR Grimsargh terminus and the PLR The original booking office for the P&L Grimsargh Station is shown at the west side of the Plough Inn. David Hindle

The former LMS Grimsargh station building was immortalised by the aptly named street, 'Old Station Close', where my parents' bungalow was built from recycled granite from the former station. It, therefore, provides a personal legacy to both the railway and to the memory of my late parents, Joan and Norman Hindle (shown here at their front door). David Hindle

CHAPTER TEN

A Miscellany of Personal Recollections

As we have seen the Longridge line closed to passengers in 1930 and partially (at Longridge) to freight in 1967. This concluding chapter features the personal recollections of passengers, railwaymen and those who knew it well. While wallowing in unashamed nostalgia, we begin with the memories of an actual passenger. At the beginning of a new millennium and over 70 years after he last used the passenger service, young Nick Swarbrick, by now a sprightly 107-year-old, and extremely eloquent venerable gentleman, spoke of the steep gradients and the once-abundant corncrake acting as an alarm clock to prompt him to get up and to catch the Longridge to Preston train – an altogether different world. 'From my garden at Blackrock Farm, Grimsargh, I watched the trains struggling up the steep gradients. The slipping of the engine's wheels were hastened by wet and frosty weather and on occasions, freight trains had to uncouple with half their train and then return from Longridge yard for the other half. At Blackrock Farm the fascinating rasping call of the now long-gone corncrake from deep within the hay meadows served as an alarm clock for me to get up and catch the 8am train to school at Preston. We did not need to go out of the house until the train was in Grimsargh station. When the train coasted down the gradient from Longridge and the crossing gates closed that was the signal for me to walk onto the platform. My neighbour, Margaret Mallott from Grimsargh House, alighted at Deepdale station to attend the girls' grammar (Park School) whilst I went onto Preston station for the Catholic grammar school'.

Time had stood still in Grimsargh until the railway began to impact on this essentially agricultural community. In those peaceful days around the turn of the twentieth century, the local traffic on Long Sight Lane constituted a few horses and traps, the odd traction engine, and the herds of cattle and flocks of sheep that were driven all the way from local farms to Preston Cattle Market, but nevertheless the insularity of the local rural community at Grimsargh had its moments of outrage.

Margaret Finch recalled that, during the roaring twenties when she was barely ten years old, she was sent with some clogs to the wooden cobbler's shop next to the Plough Inn. What transpired had such a profound effect on her that she ran to her home to Long Sight Lane to recall the choice language used by an errant Grimsargh farmer. As the level crossing gates made their customary clank across Long Sight Lane to give the morning passenger train the road to Longridge, a herdsman was driving his cattle home and was stopped in his tracks. The farmer did not mince his words: 'You shitten-arsed bugger!' – clearly a very articulate man – this was directed at the humble porter for allowing the train to proceed. One could say that he remonstrated with the porter, but, in charting the social history of events, is it not better to use the actual colourful language of this down-to-earth local? I am reliably informed that the abuse could have been much worse and, by normal standards, it was a term of endearment.

In more tranquil moments during the 1920s, Margaret paid a penny for a bar of Nestlé's chocolate from the machine on Grimsargh Station, before catching the train to Preston to see a music hall performance at the old Empire Theatre on Church Street. It certainly made a change from the 'Physic Revellers' and amateur plays and pantomime on offer at the old 'tin tabernacle', more politely known as the Grimsargh Assembly Rooms.

Three of Grimsargh's respected elderly gentlemen kept one another company on the wooden bench next to the station. From this strategic position they had been watching the world go by since, it seemed, time immemorial. Matters of all sorts were debated at length and judgements handed down; the person or persons being discussed going about their daily lives in blissful ignorance of

WD 'Austerity' Class 8F 2-8-0 No. 90675 at Courtaulds on 22 August 1964, with the fireman operating the ground frame and the escape siding to the right. Courtesy: Alan Castle

the 'rulings from the bench'. One day in the late 1930s, they had a matter of extreme gravity to cope with, when the peaceful tranquillity of Grimsargh was completely shattered. There was no opportunity for stops at Grimsargh Station when a runaway train smashed through the level crossing gates and had to be diverted up a specially constructed steep escape route at Courtaulds' Sidings. The wagons were finally consigned to an ignominious end in the local scrap-yard, while any unfortunate villagers witnessing the spectacle were prescribed to a minimum of twelve months counselling!

During the 'swinging sixties', Martin Willacy was employed at Longridge Station as a clerk in the parcels' office. The following account is based on his personal experiences: 'Work in the parcels office on Longridge station during the early 1960s provided an insight into the workings of the branch. In the 1950s, the Preston to Longridge branch had up to four freight trains per day between Monday-Friday and two on Saturday. Engines from Preston shed (code 10B) worked them all, except the afternoon one which was worked by an ex-L&YR Aspinall Class 3F 0-6-0 from Lostock Hall (code 24C). The others were worked by ex-LNWR 7F 0-8-0s and BR Class 2MT 2-6-0s. The second one of the day worked through to Longridge, with the remaining three terminated at Courtaulds' Exchange Sidings.

'By the late 1950s, the Longridge line was frequently diagrammed for a Mold Junction, Chester (code 6B) Stanier Class Five 2-6-0. There were also occasional appearances of Hughes Fowler (Crab) Class Five 2-6-0s, Stanier Class Five 4-6-0s, Stanier 8F 2-8-0s and WD 2-8-0s. In about 1959, a number of Stanier Class 5 2-6-0s were allocated to Preston shed (by then code 24K) and one was

'Jubilee' Class 6P5F 4-6-0 No. 45604 'Ceylon' was an unusual visitor to Longridge in 1961, consigned to working the daily freight. Courtesy: Martin Willacy

WD 'Austerity' class
2-8-0 No. 90675
approaches the closed
crossing gates at
Grimsargh Station *en
route* to Longridge
on 22 August 1964.
Courtesy: Alan Castle

A solitary member
of the station staff
emerges from the goods
and parcels office at
Longridge Station to
observe WD 'Austerity'
class 2-8-0 No. 90675
hauling its train to
the goods yard on 22
August 1964. Courtesy:
Alan Castle

A rare visitor to
Courtaulds' Exchange
Sidings, in September
1961, was Class 3F
'Jinty' 0-6-0T No
47572. Courtesy: John
Holmes

diagrammed for Longridge. In 1960, Preston engine-shed was burnt down and closed – most of the remaining locomotives being sent to Lostock Hall. By 1962, the morning Longridge run was diagrammed for a Carnforth (24L) Stanier Class "5" 4-6-0. However, about once a week, former "Jubilee" Class 6P5F 4-6-0 express passenger engines, relegated to goods duties, were seen at Longridge, including No. 45604 "Ceylon". By 1962, the load was typically between two and ten goods wagons, with most of the traffic being coal and agricultural produce.

'At Longridge station, clerical work for the goods traffic was undertaken and tickets from Preston station were issued between 9am and 5pm. Parcels were despatched via a road van for forwarding by rail from Preston, either by passenger train or goods van. This was called "Sundry traffic." A road van based in the old L&YR yard at Preston Butler Street came out every morning to Longridge. This vehicle carried parcels which had arrived at Preston by goods train and then carried out a delivery service around the Longridge district, returning to Preston at the end of the day.

At this time the stationmaster in charge of Longridge was a Mr. Unsworth, whose main office was at Barton and Broughton. This station on the main line had a small goods yard close to the old passenger station that closed in 1939. The yard was served by a daily pick-up goods train, which ran from Preston to Garstang Town and Pilling, the so-called "Pilling Pig".' [97]

John Holmes of Longridge (a past member of the Ian Allan Loco Spotters club) has kindly provided his original notes appertaining to the PLR during the early 1960s and to which some additional detail has been provided in respect of locomotive allocations, etc: 'On 25th January 1960, Stanier Class 8F No 48771 came up to Longridge with the usual morning goods train and returned to Preston. At 11am the same day a special working saw Preston Shed's Stanier Class 5 No 45454 with a breakdown train to attend to a derailment in Longridge yard. The breakdown train had difficulty getting up the gradient at Stone Bridge and slipped to a standstill once, before eventually reaching the Longridge goods yard. At mid-day, No 45454 went back to Preston light-engine. At 3.30pm un-rebuilt "Patriot" Class 6P5F 4-6-0 No 45502 "Royal Naval Division" came up to Longridge, light-engine to shunt the breakdown crane, before returning to Preston about 5 o'clock the same day. This was probably the only visit ever of a "Patriot" locomotive to Longridge.

'The afternoon train, visiting Grimsargh goods yard on 28th April 1960, produced the surprising appearance of Fairburn 2-6-4T No 42210, which had probably been "borrowed" during its transfer from Scotland's 67D Ardrossan shed to 6C Birkenhead. On 29th June 1960, Class 4F 0-6-0 No 44237 was seen on the branch originating from 8B Warrington shed. Another rare visitor on the branch was 26F Patricroft's Standard Class 5MT 4-6-0 No 73044 on 14th July 1963. The only time that I ever encountered a class 3F 0-6-0T "Jinty" was in September 1961. It was Lostock Hall-based No 47572.

'On 15th May 1960, the so called "dandelion express," sprayed the track with weed-killer at Grimsargh. The train was hauled by Wakefield shed's WD "Austerity" 2-8-0 No 90361 and consisted of a green 1st class Southern carriage, several old ex-Midland tenders containing the weed-killer and a guard's van. Throughout July 1960, a substantial length of track was re-laid on either side of Grimsargh level crossing. Locomotives engaged on the special trains included Preston shed's Stanier Class 5MT 2-6-0 No 42960 and, from the same depot, 0-6-0 diesel shunters Nos D3369, D3371 and D3846.'

The recollections of Assistant Chief Mechanical Engineer, Eric Langridge (latterly residing at Pevensey, Sussex), in a letter to Mike Atherton of Preston, dated September 1992, imply that one of the earliest experiments with prototype diesel multiple-units took place on the Longridge branch about the time of nationalisation: [98] 'Addressing my letter to you, reminded me of the time I came to Preston for a few days, riding with one or two others (who had supplied some of the equipment) on a vehicle rigged up by the English Electric Company with their first under-floor diesel engine for railcar use. As the vehicle came into Preston station, it looked like a box on wheels, there being just about enough room for six of us on board. A Mr Reid was the driver and we had an LMS pilot. We turned off up the Longridge branch, which we had to ourselves for the rest of the day. We had a good lunch near the top of the branch. That must have been before nationalisation – come to think of it, food rationing was still on. The trip gave the manufacturers the chance to see how their equipment stood up to a fairly long day's work, but the railway could only report that it was "an interesting proposal". I thought Preston, with its main high street and striking town hall (it had not been burned down then), a fine place and what a railway station – with the park alongside. Many thanks again and good wishes. Yours sincerely, Eric Langridge'.

Although this wasn't the earliest experiment with diesel railcars, it was certainly among the first. The LMS had tried various designs in the late 1920s and 1930s, but none of these appeared to meet with total success.

Contemporaneous with the gradual demise of the branch is the following anecdotal material provided by engine driver Bob Jackson, concerning freight workings at Deepdale, in the early 1960s: 'A rather amusing incident occurred on 20th March 1963, whilst working the local trip to Deepdale coal depot and Red Scar sidings at Courtaulds, both located on the steeply-graded Longridge branch. The job was now incorporated into the morning 15 Target working and could be heavily loaded with household coal and wagons for Courtaulds. My driver for the day was Sammy Waterworth, with Arthur Gilbert in the brake van of the unfitted train and an "Austerity" 2-8-0 No 90675 of Lostock Hall shed at the business end.

'The branch-line left the main line by the side of No 5 Signal Box and immediately passed Maudland yard on the left. Once on the Longridge branch, you had to let yourself into Maudland yard, via a manually-operated ground frame. Once unlocked, you could take out the single-line token key for the branch and, whilst you had this token in your possession, no other train could use the branch, until you returned to Maudland.

'On the day in question, we had had a full load, and ran onto the 1 in 54 gradient, and into the 862 yards long Maudland Tunnel. The locomotive was down to a crawl in the tunnel and both the heat and smoke were almost unbearable, as Sammy asked if the boiler was O.K. I replied that the boiler water level was just over three quarters full and the fire well built-up with steam on full pressure. By this time, we were just over half-way through the tunnel when he told me to get off the footplate and to walk and climb back aboard once the engine emerged into the daylight. This I did, and I noticed that Sammy was walking behind me. There was nobody on the footplate!

'Sammy explained that all we had to do was wait for the locomotive and re-board. We could still hear the beat of the engine working very hard, but strangely it appeared to be going away from us. After remarking on this, Sammy replied, "Rubbish, it will come out any second", but it never did. The weight of the train had caused the train to slip, pulling it back into Maudland yard. Luckily, the guard, realising the train was out of control, applied the handbrake in his van, averting what could have been a major incident, but got a real shock when he found no men on the footplate. Walking back to Maudland through the tunnel with no light was even worse than sticking it out on the engine. Sam got a severe reprimand for his actions but, somehow, managed to talk his way out of it.'

'Another amusing incident happened a couple of years later, involving driver Harry Ridding on the same working with "Austerity" No 90720. That day, there was no traffic for Courtaulds, and with only the Deepdale coal to haul the train was lightly-loaded. All went well until we reached Deepdale junction. After a few blasts on the whistle, we noticed that there was still no movement from the signal box. As the box operated the level crossing gates for the main road, we assumed that there must be a build-up of road traffic and, as we were running early, the signalman had decided to clear the backlog before accepting us. Some five minutes later, there was still no sign of us moving, so to the box we went. On his desk was a note saying that he had "gone to Signal 43". This had to be some sort of code, as his total signals only amounted to six. "Right," said Harry, "you go back on the footplate and I'll open the gates to the railway and set the points. When you see the ground signal come off, bring the train up over the crossing and I'll put you into the coal yard". This I did, as Harry stayed in the box. After shunting the loaded wagons in and the empties out, I took the train back over the crossing. Harry set the points back down the branch and came back to the footplate to take the train back to the North Union yard at Preston. It was whilst awaiting relief that I mentioned to Harry what a brilliant idea I thought it was to operate the box ourselves. A look of horror came over his face and he replied, "My God, I've forgotten to put the gates back!"' [99]

A Retrospective Footplate Ride on the PLR

My own fondest memory of the Longridge branch was when I rode on the footplate of the last steam locomotive from Courtaulds to Lostock Hall, on Friday, 2 August 1968, which also marked the last day of full-scale steam freight operations on British Railways and was the penultimate day before the official cessation of steam. The train was unceremoniously hauled by an unkempt former Carnforth engine in the form of Stanier Class 5 4-6-0 No 44874 and proved to be the final occasion upon which a steam locomotive would traverse the old PLR metals. This particular engine had just been transferred to Lostock Hall depot from Carnforth, to be used as motive power on one of the six enthusiasts' specials operating on the final day of official steam working – Sunday, 4 August 1968. It would never return to its home shed.

The grand finale of steam heralded the closure of the last three remaining engine-sheds on the BR network, at Carnforth, Rose Grove and Lostock Hall, and the blanket scrapping of steam locomotives. The following day, Lostock Hall shed became a morgue for rows of condemned locomotives. Recalling those great days of steam are a few photographs taken of the locomotive and from the footplate on that special day.

The end of an era was unceremoniously recorded on the Longridge line on Friday, 2 August 1968, when one of the last grimy Stanier Class Fives, No. 44874, from Carnforth shed (10A) worked a train to Courtaulds' Exchange Sidings, along the former branch line. It is seen here at Ribbleton, on the down working, passing under Blackpool Road Bridge preceeding the junction with the branch to the banana warehouse (right). Courtesy: Chris Spring

Running tender-first, No. 44874 makes the final approach to Courtaulds' on 2 August 1968, just two days before the very end of steam on British Railways. Colloquially speaking, the Stanier Class 5 has reached the end of the line and two days later, the locomotive's fire would be dropped for the very last time. David Hindle

Stanier Class 5 4-6-0 No. 44874 alongside Courtaulds' No. 2 ground frame with the very last steam engine to operate over PLR metals. David Hindle

Left: Close-up of No. 44874 at Courtaulds, suitably embellished with the words 'Goodbye, but not forgotten' and the number 44874 scrufily painted on the front. Courtesy: Chris Spring

Below: Perpetual motion but not for much longer – close up of the Stanier Class 5 4-6-0 wheel arrangement. The locomotive is about to set off along the branch from Ribbleton to Preston. Courtesy: Alan Middleton

No. 44874 gains the double tracks at Deepdale Junction, to pass under the ornate Deepdale Mill Street Bridge. David Hindle

The driver's view as Stanier Class 5 No. 44874 crosses over the canal bridge at Maudland. David Hindle

No. 44874 passes the now-demolished platforms of the East Lancashire line at Preston Station and heads towards the last steam MPD at Lostock Hall. David Hindle

Appendices

Appendix I

A Brief Chronological History of the Preston to Longridge railway

Year	Name of Event
1836	The Royal Assent is granted by Parliament to the Preston & Longridge Railway Company.
1840	The line opens and services commence between Longridge and Deepdale Street stations – the latter being the initial terminus of the line. Initially, horse-haulage is adopted.
1846	The entire line is leased to the Fleetwood, Preston & West Riding Junction Railway (FP&WRR).
1848	The first steam-hauled train runs on Whit Monday.
1850	A double-track extension now connects the existing line, a few hundred yards east of the Deepdale Street terminus at Deepdale Junction, with Maudland and thence onto the existing route into the Fylde, via the new Maudland (or 'Miley') tunnel. Freight traffic only is conveyed at this time.
1854	A new station is opened at what is successively to be named Gamull (or Gammer) Lane in 1854, Fulwood in 1856 and, ultimately, Ribbleton in 1900. (The latter not to be confused with the later Ribbleton Station that came to be situated nearby.)
1856	The passenger line is extended, with new stations being opened at Deepdale and Maudland Bridge, the latter being at the Werstern (new) end of the line and close to Preston town centre.
1863	A new station is opened at Ribbleton. (Not to be confused with the earlier built station that came to assume the name following closure of the later establishment!)
1867	The LNWR & LYR Joint Committee assumes ownership and operation of the line from the FP&WRR.
1868	The 1863 Ribbleton Station is closed to all traffic.
1870	The latter-day Grimsargh Station is opened for business, replacing the earlier structure located within the premises of the Plough Inn.
1872	A new station at Longridge is built adjacent to the Towneley Arms Hotel.
1885	The installation is completed of the Maudland Curve that provided the direct link to Preston Station and facilitating railway connections to other railway lines to the south for the first time. Concurrently with this, Maudland Bridge Station is closed.
1889	The Whittingham Hospital Railway was opened and commenced a passenger service connecting into the Longridge services.
1923	Following the 'Grouping', the London Midland & Scottish Railway assumes ownership and operation of the line from the LNWR & LYR Joint Committee.
1948	Following 'Nationalisation', British Railways takes over operation of the line.

1930 After 90 years, passenger services are withdrawn from the entire line, as from 2 June 1930, causing the closure of all stations to passengers – although freight and parcels traffic will survive for much longer.

1957 The Whittingham Hospital Railway is closed to all traffic; its passenger services having survived those on the 'main-line' by all of 27 years!

1967 The withdrawal of freight facilities at Grimsargh and Longridge stations, in November 1967, brings about the complete closure of the route beyond Courtaulds' Sidings.

1980 Courtaulds' Factory closes and, with it, the section of line between Courtaulds' Sidings and Deepdale Junction.

1994 The withdrawal of the final coal trains serving Deepdale brings about the complete closure of the remaining operable section of the line.

Appendix II

FPWRJR ACT, 1846 – Scale of Charges

The following provides an overview of the nature of goods carried by the railway and the scale of charges for both the carriage of freight and passengers. Supplements were also payable in respect of certain goods carried by the Company and, if engines were used for drawing or propelling trucks, an extra three farthings was to be charged for both passengers and all classes of inanimate freight. The Company was also to abide by Acts of Parliament already passed in references to the conveyance of mail and troops.

We begin with the charges for the carriage of passengers in 1846: 'First-class carriage passenger travel not to be more than tuppence per mile; second-class carriages with glass windows and fully closed – three half pennies per mile; third-class carriages – one penny per mile. Dung, compost manure, lime, limestone, road repairing materials – three farthings per ton per mile. Coal, coke, charcoal, cinders, stones, bricks, slate, clay and iron-ore – one penny per ton per mile. Sugar, grain, corn, flour, hides, timber, stones, anvils, vices and chain – half penny per ton per mile. Cottons, wools, manufactured goods, dead fish, dead poultry – tuppence a mile per ton. Carriages of more than two wheels and not weighing more than one and a half tons – five pence per mile. Horses, mules, asses – three pence per mile, cows and cattle – half penny per mile, calves, sheep, pigs, lambs and dogs – farthing per mile.'

Appendix III

Important Sale of Railway Plant Advertised in the Preston and Lancashire Chronicle on 8 September 1849

'To be sold by auction:

At the Station of the Lancaster & Preston Junction Railway at Lancaster on the Tuesday 18th September, next, and the following days, until the whole be sold: the sale of locomotives engines and tenders, carriages, materials and other plant of the said Lancaster & Preston Junction Railway Company (that company having ceased to work their railway since the 1st August instant, when their arrangements with the Lancaster & Carlisle Railway Company came into operation) including an entirely new Travelling Post Office, built to correspond in every respect with those used on the LNWR, six locomotive engines, seven 1st class carriages, six 2nd class carriages, five 3rd class carriages, eight carriage trucks, three luggage vans, one goods van, five horse boxes, twenty-nine goods wagons, extra wheels, tools, office furniture, etc. The whole may be viewed at the said Station and catalogues may be had on application to the Secretary, on and after Wednesday, the 29th August instant. By order R.C. Rawlinson, Secretary, Lancaster, 22nd August, 1849.'

As explained in Chapter 3, for its own use, the PLR was successful in bidding for several of these locomotives and items of rolling stock.

Appendix IV

'Auction sale on Monday 14th June 1852 of FP&WRR equipment under distress for rent. Sold without reserve for ready money. [100]

At Longridge Station:

The whole of the railway materials, consisting of two railway engines and tenders in good working order, first, second and third-class carriages, stone wagons, large travelling hoisting crane, with chains and large iron dogs and chains, three single hoisting cranes and chains, four lots of iron railway chairs, lots of old iron, three turntables, grindstone, several lots of wagon wheels, new oak carriage frame, porter's truck and several lots of brass steps. Longridge quarry – large powerful travelling crane, chains and hoisting tackle; to other single hoisting cranes and tackle.

At Grimsargh Station:

Railway plates, irons and chains, two stoves and piping, office desk, forms, ladder, large oil lamp and grates'.

As explained in Chapter Three, the stock listed above was transferred to the P.L.R. in lieu of outstanding rent due and the latter resumed operation of the line as from 15 November 1852.

Appendix V

Extracts from the Report carried out by Colonel W. Yolland into the Railway Accident at Fulwood, which occurred on 10th August 1867

'The PLR is a single-line of about seven miles in length … There are two intermediate Stations at Fulwood and Grimsargh respectively, which are provided with low disc signals at the platforms and used as Station signals and put on at danger when any passengers are waiting at those Stations to proceed either by the up or down trains. There are no distant signals at those Stations.

'The usual traffic is limited to about four trains in each direction daily, except on Saturdays, where there are five; but, of late years, special or excursion trains have been run between Preston (Deepdale Goods Station) and Longridge, about ten times in the course of each season, and these excursion trains have been interpolated to run between the ordinary trains. From the nature of the inclines between Preston and Longridge, the return excursion trains from Longridge to Preston have usually been attached to the ordinary trains, one engine being sufficient to take both trains; and on these occasions the engine taking the excursion train to Longridge has returned empty to Preston.

'Excursion trains were advertised to run from Preston to Longridge on Saturday the 10th ultimo for the Longridge Guild, at 3, 4, and 5.45pm and Mr Walmsley, formerly the secretary, but now the superintendent of the line, looked after the working of the traffic, and about 2,200 passengers altogether were taken to Longridge. An excursion train also followed the last ordinary train from Preston on Saturday the 10th ultimo at 7.30pm, both trains reaching Longridge shortly after 8pm. Mr Walmsley directed that the excursion train should not be attached to the ordinary train due to leave Longridge at 8.30pm, but should precede it; and this excursion train, consisting of an engine and tender, running tender foremost, 13 carriages and a brake van left Longridge at 8.25pm according to the superintendent of the line and the guard of the train, with instructions to stop at Grimsargh and Fulwood to collect tickets.

'Prior to this train leaving Longridge, the engine driver informed the superintendent that he had no tail lights on to his train, and was answered that as the ordinary would not return to Longridge he would not want them. The guard states that he also asked for taillight but did not get them.

'The excursion train stopped about five minutes at Grimsargh Station, and next pulled up at Fulwood Station, where there is a low platform on the western side of the line, about 75 yards in length, and a Station house occupied by a platelayer, who works on the line during the day, while his daughter has charge of the Station in his absence, issues tickets and turns on the disc signal to danger for a train to stop when passengers want to be taken on, but she cannot be said to be in the employment of the Company as she is not paid. The taxes of the house are paid, and the platelayer is allowed a piece of garden ground, as is paid 2s 6d per week in addition to his wages as a platelayer for taking care of the Station. On Saturdays he is allowed to leave his regular work at 4pm.

'When the excursion train stopped at Fulwood Station, a little before 9pm, the brakes were put on, on the tender and brake van, which stood next to the engine in front of the Station, as the Station is, I am informed, constructed on an incline of 1 in 75, and the train is said to have been there for five or six minutes, during which time the tickets were being collected, when the ordinary train from Longridge, consisting of an engine and tender, running tender first, 17 carriages and one brake van arrived, and ran into the rear carriage of the excursion train, which stood about 10 yards north of the Station platform, at a speed estimated at from 5 to 7 miles and hour, and threw it off the line.

'The disc signal at Fulwood Station can be seen for nearly three quarters of a mile from a train approaching from Longridge. On this occasion it showed and was observed as a white light, so that it was, in the absence of any tail lights in the excursion train, a positive indication that the ordinary train need not stop at Fulwood Station, for any purpose, although it was intended to do so; and the driver did not observe that there was a train standing at Fulwood Station until he was about 125 yards from it – to late too stop short of it. The effect of the collision was to destroy the carriages, which stood next to the brake van at the front of the excursion train, and to greatly damage the carriage at the rear of the same train, and to knock a hole in the tender of the ordinary train that struck the last carriage.

'I have not been enabled to learn precisely at what time the collision took place, as the Station is not provided with any clock, nor the guards with any watches. The platelayer in charge of the Station had a hand lamp with him while the tickets were being collected, and one of the guards of the excursion train, of which there were two, states that he took it out of the platelayer's hand for the purpose of showing a red light to the ordinary train just before the collision took place, but the lamp was not furnished with a red glass; and although he said he waved the lamp up and down the driver of the ordinary train does not appear to have noticed it.

'This collision has resulted from the absence of proper arrangements for conducting passenger traffic, and I consider it to be entirely due to the mismanagement of the superintendent and not to that of the drivers or guards of the trains, or the platelayer in charge of the Station. I have never met with a similar case. The line would not now be passed as a passenger line, with a Station or Stations on steep incline, on which carriages will not stand, and where there are not precautions adopted for preventing carriages from running away, and which is not provided with proper signals or even a Station-master.

'The line now belongs to two powerful railway companies, and it is not creditable to their management that such defective arrangements should have been permitted to continue undisturbed for a year after it had come into their possession. Their passenger traffic is exceedingly large, and the best means of working it is now thoroughly understood; but this collision only adds another instance to the many on record, that the public safety is often not properly cared for until the necessity for alterations in the mode of working traffic has been proved by the occurrence of some serious accident.

W. Yolland, (Colonel)
The Secretary of the Board of Trade, Railway Department'.

Appendix VI

A Representative Selection of Steam Locomotives Recorded on the PLR during the 1950/60s

Hughes-Fowler Class 5MT 2-6-0 42722, 42848 and 42900	Stanier Class 5MT 2-6-0 42960, 42965 and 42976
Super D Class 7F 0-8-0 49104, 49141, 49191, 49267, 49382, 49390, 49391, 49396 and 49451	Aspinall Class 3F 0-6-0 52182, 52290, 52336, 52368, 52429, 52445, 52456, 52458 and 52526
Stanier Class 5MT 4-6-0 44384, 44681, 44958, 44971, 44874, 45150 45212, 45315, 45110 and 44761	Stanier Class 8F 2-8-0 48002, 48237, 48338, 48438, 48476, 48478, 48669, 48707 and 48774
'Jubilee' Class '6P5F' 4-6-0 45604 'Ceylon, '45625 'Sarawak,' 45696 'Arethusa' and 45633 'Aden.'	Unrebuilt 'Patriot' Class 6P5F 4-6-0 No 45502 'Royal Naval Division'
Ivatt Class 2MT 2-6-0 46414, 46429, 46430, 46447 Standard Class 5MT 4-6-0 and 2MT 2-6-0 73044, 78036 and 78037	WD 'Austerity' Class 8F 2-8-0 90183, 90566, 90631, 90658, 90675 and 90681

Appendix VII

Principal Bridges and Tunnels

Type	No	Location
Road bridge over railway	1	Maudland Bank, Preston
Railway over canal	2	Lancaster Canal
Road bridge over railway	3	Cold Bath Street
-do-	4	Pollard Street
-do-	5	Radnor Street
-do-	6	Fylde Road
No 1 tunnel	7	Adelphi Street
No 2 tunnel	8	Moor Lane
No 3 tunnel	9	North Road
Road bridge over railway	10	St Paul's Road
-do-	11	Deepdale Road
-do	12	Deepdale Road Station
Foot bridge over railway	12A	Porter Street footbridge
-do-	12B	Deepdale Mill Street
-do-	12C	Blackpool Road
-do-	13	Cromwell Road
Culvert	14	Eaves Brook
Footbridge over railway	14A	Gamull Lane
Road bridge over railway	15	Gamull Lane

Footbridge over railway	15A	Sulby Drive
Bridge over motorway	15B	M6
Occupation bridge	16	Church House, Grimsargh
Foot bridge over railway	16A	Adjacent Preston Road
Road bridge over railway	17	Preston Road, Grimsargh
Short tunnel	18	Four Lane Ends Longridge
Occupation Bridges	19, 20, 21	Quarry Extension
Tunnel	22	Entrance to Quarries

Appendix VIII

Signalling on the Preston to Longridge Railway

The Preston to Longridge railway was signalled by standard LNWR equipment from new. Initially it was signalled as a passenger line, hence the elaborate arrangements.

Signal Boxes

- Longridge cabin opened in 1884, 9-foot square LNWR standard Type 4-timber superstructure on brick base with Saxby & Farmer lever frame. [101] (11 levers).
- Deepdale Junction cabin was a standard Type 4 cabin timber superstructure with a brick base size 'H'. [102] 23-lever LNWR tumbler frame. [103]
- Maudland Curve cabin was a 20-lever LNWR frame (type unknown), all-timber structure size 'D'.

Level Crossings

- Longridge; Grimsargh; Deepdale Goods (Deepdale Mill Street) Worked by hand, released by Annett's lock by train staff, gates interlocked were with signals
- Deepdale junction (Skeffington Road) worked from the signal box, full interlocking with signals.

Ground Frames

All released by Annett's Lock/train staff – configuration 'A', generally interlocked by lug locking*.

- Longridge for the goods yard and the sidings at Longridge quarry.
- Grimsargh for the goods yard and the asylum railway.
- Cold-storage depot (2 levers)
- Croft's Sidings (2 levers)
- Martin's Siding (2 levers)
- Courtaulds Nos 1 and 2 Sidings (2 Levers)
- Deepdale Goods (8 Levers)

---

* In railway signalling, an Annett's key is a large key that locks levers or other items of signalling apparatus, thereby functioning as a portable form of interlocking. When not in use, the key is normally held in an Annett's lock that is fixed to the lever or apparatus concerned. With the key removed from the lock, the lever or apparatus is locked and cannot be moved. The keys and locks are given a matching configuration to prevent keys of a different configuration being inserted into the wrong lock.

Line Operation

- Tootle Heights to Longridge level crossing – worked as a single goods line (1349 yds) with no block or bells. [104]
- Longridge level crossing to Deepdale Junction – worked as a single goods line [105] (5 miles 922 yds), using a round staff of colour red, known as 'one engine in steam'.
- Deepdale Junction to Deepdale Goods (750 yds) – worked as a single-line & loop line, with no block or bell. [106]
- Deepdale Junction to Maudland Curve (1 mile 406 yds) – worked as up & down goods lines.
- Maudland Curve and Preston No 5 Signal Box (300 yds) – worked as up & down good's lines. [107]

Facing Point Locks

When passenger trains passed over points from the switch end (facing) direction, Board of Trade regulations stipulated that the points must be locked in position to prevent them moving under traffic.

Special Features at Deepdale Junction

A train arriving from Longridge and approaching Deepdale would 'whistle' when one mile away and the first signal the driver would see would be the distant. The next signal seen would be the Deepdale Junction home signal. Upon arrival at the signal, if this was at danger, then there was a 'FCB' (fireman's call box) to use. This contained a button or plunger that the fireman would press, which would sound a bell and show an indication in the signal box that a train was waiting at the signal.

Speed Limits

- The maximum speed limit from Longridge to Deepdale Junction – 25 mph.
- Reduced maximum speed limit – 15 mph between Deepdale Goods and Deepdale Junction. [108]
- 10mph through junctions and over curves between Maudland Curve and Preston No 5 Signal Box.

Special Instructions

These were special instructions stated for the operation of the line in the LM&SR Sectional Appendix for the Western Division March 1937:

Chapel Hill, Asylum, Grimsargh Goods Yard, Courtaulds' and Croft's Siding:

'Trains must not be shunted into sidings for trains to pass', which would strictly enforce the 'one engine in steam' mode of operation.

Longridge Goods Yard:

'Guards must not detach wagons from the engine until they have been brought to a stand, and secured by side brakes or sprags as necessary.' [109]

Grimsargh Level Crossing:

'Normal position of gates is across the railway and are operated by porter until 5:30pm. Any train working through the crossing after 5:30pm must stop at Deepdale Junction Signal Box for guard to obtain key of gates, which must be returned to the signalman on return journey.' [110]

Courtaulds' Nos 1 and 2 Sidings:

'Ground Frame, controlled by train staff. When wagons are attached, or detached, the whole train must first be placed in the lie-by siding adjacent to the main line, through the points at the Longridge end of the sidings.' [111]

Bibliography

Primary Sources including British Transport Historical Records held at The National Archive, Kew

Reference	Title	Covering dates
Rail 1075/428	Prospectus: Preston & Longridge Railway	1835
ZPER 33/1	Description of Line (Railway Mag. Vol. 1)	1836
Rail 410/1145	Map of Preston to Longridge Branch	1843-1957
Rail 207/2	FP&WRR Minutes of Board Meetings	1857-1868
ZPER 34/20	The Illustrated London News	1852
Rail 576	Minutes of the Preston – Longridge Joint Committee	1866-1889
Rail 981/96	FP&WRR Summer Timetable	1866
Rail 1053/58	Colonel Yolland's P.L.R. accident report	1867
MT 6/482/6	Grimsargh Level Crossing	1887
Rail 795/16	Contract between L&YR/LNWR & HM Postmaster	1888
Rail 405/61	Preston – Longridge, Widening at Preston Station	1899
Rail 329	Whittingham Railway	1887-1957
AN 155/14	Preston – Longridge	1964-1968

Primary Sources held at the Lancashire Record Office

LRO PDR58	Enclosure Awards	1835
LRO DDC1/1183	Original correspondence of P & L Railway	1836
LRO DDCL1187/2	Notice of Meeting to raise Money for P & L Rly	1840
LRO DDX1162/3	Correspondence regarding FP&WRR Extension to Hellifield	1914/24
LRO DDX3/110	Excess fare ticket	1850
LRO PDR243	Map of P & L Railway showing townships	1835
LRO PDR460	Map of P & L Railway (brittle)	1845
LRO DP432/52	Map of P & L Railway 4 miles east Grimsargh	1884
LRO DDX189/15	Original plan of route of WHR	1884
LRO DDX189/16	Parliamentary procedures - plan of WHR	1885
LRO NC Ac. 8276 Box 87	Photograph of N.C.B. Sidings, Preston (NCB Photo Library Neg 9598)	c. 1950s
LRO HRW1/6	Whittingham Sub Committee Minute Books	

Primary Sources held at the National Railway Museum, York

PR40-E2   Preston to Longridge Timetables: 1870/75/81/82/84/91

Primary Sources held at Greater Manchester County Record Office

A19/4/903   Joint L&YR/LNWR and BR bridge plans   1913-1958

Secondary Sources

Books

Biddle, G. *The Railways Around Preston – A Historical Review* (Foxline Publishing) 1989
Bowtell, H. D. *Lesser Railways of Bowland Forest and Craven Country* (Plateway Press) 1988
Castle, A. G. *Steam – The Grand Finale* (Morton Publishing) 2008
Clinker, C. R. *Railway History Sources* (AO4CC1)
Hindle, D. *Grimsargh: The Story of a Lancashire Village* (Carnegie Publishing) 2002
Holt, G. *Regional History of Railways in Great Britain, Vol X* (David & Charles) 1979
Jackson, B. *Steaming Ambitions* (Triangle Publishing) 1999
Marshall, J. *Lancashire & Yorkshire Railway, Vols. 1&3* (David & Charles) 1969
Parker, N. *The Preston & Longridge Railway* (Oakwood Press) 1972
Pennie, R. *John Ramsbottom, Victorian Engineer* (L&YR Society) 2008
Reed, B. *Crewe to Carlisle* (Ian Allan) 1969
Rush, R. W. *The L&YR and its Locomotives, 1846-1923* (London, 1949)
Smith, T. *A History of Longridge* (Longridge, 1888)
Till, J. M. *A History of Longridge and its People* (Carnegie Publishing) 1993

Periodicals

Greville, H. D. 'The Railways of Lancashire', *Transactions of the Historic Society of Lancashire and Cheshire*, Volume 105, 1953
Greville & Holt. 'Railway Development in Preston', *Railway Magazine*, March 1960
Hilbert, M. 'Coal to Deepdale No More' *Traction*, April 1998
Hindle, D. 'Grimsargh Junction, Change For Whittingham', *Steam Days*, May 2004
Perkins, T. R. 'The Whittingham Railway', *Railway Magazine*, April 1934

Endnotes

1   'Bandsmen of Yesterday', by Harry Clegg, *Longridge News & Advertiser,* October 1968
2   Smith T. *History of Longridge,* p.44
3   Till, J.M. *A History of Longridge and its People,* (Carnegie Publishing 1993) p 114
4   *Preston Guardian,* 28 March 1885,
5   Hewitson A. *History of Preston,* 1883 pp. 203/6
6   *Preston Chronicle* 2 September 1837
7   *Preston Pilot* 18 July 1840
8   Hewitson, A. *History of Preston,* (Preston, 1883) pp.195-209
9   Rail, 1075/428, The National Archive, Kew
10 LRO DDC1/1183 and Commercial directory of Preston, 1841 p. 110.
11 *Preston Pilot,* 21 April 1838
12 *Preston Chronicle,* 2 May 1840
13 Smith T. *History of Longridge,* (Longridge, 1888) p.42
14 *Featured on the 6 in. to one mile OS map of 1849.*
15 *Preston Chronicle,* 25 April 1840
16 *Commercial directory of Preston, 1841 p. 110.*
17 *See Ordnance Survey Map, (1844) 62 to mile in L.R.O.*
18 *Mannex Directory, 1851.*
19 *Oakey's Preston Directory, 1853*
20 *Barrett's Preston Directory, 1882*
21 *Barrett's Preston Directory, 1926*
22 *The Commercial Directory of Preston, 1841, p.110*
23 *Preston Chronicle,* 2 May 1840
24 Hewitson, A. *History of Preston,* p.205
25 Hewitson, A. *History of Preston,* p.205
26 *Preston Pilot,* 24 January 1846
27 *Preston Pilot,* 13 June 1840
28 *Preston Pilot,* 29 May 1841
29 *Preston Chronicle,* 5 June 1841
30 *Preston Pilot,* 24 May 1845
31 *Preston Pilot,* 16 May 1846
32 *Rail, 576,* The National Archive, Kew
33 *Preston Chronicle,* 23 January 1847
34 Smith T. *History of Longridge,* (Longridge 1888) p.42
35 *Preston Guardian,* 17 June 1848

36 See page for full *Preston Pilot* Report of 17 June 1848
37 *Preston Guardian,* October 1849
38 *Preston Guardian,* 7 June 1851
39 *Illustrated London News,* June 1852, p. 439
40 *Rail, 576,* The National Archive, Kew
41 Hewitson A. *History of Preston,* 1883 p.205
42 *Rail 576, Item 188,* The National Archive, Kew
43 *Preston Pilot,* 11 June 1859
44 *Rail 207/2,* The National Archive, Kew
45 *Rush, R.W. The Lancashire and Yorkshire Railway and its Locomotives,* London, 1949 pp. 35-36
46 *Rail 207/2* The National Archive, Kew
47 *Rail 576,* The National Archive, Kew
48 *Rail 576, Items 485,507* The National Archive, Kew
49 *Lloyd J. List of railway Locomotives built by Beyer Peacock,* (N.R.M, 19990) p.12
50 *Pennie, R. John Ramsbottom, Victorian Engineer* (LYR Society, 2008) p.23
51 *Rail 576, Item 21,* The National Archive, Kew
52 *Preston Guardian,* 14 August 1867
53 Smith T. *History of Longridge,* (1888) p. 43. (a list of injured passengers is shown in appendix)
54 *Gr..Man. CRO A19/4/903*
55 *Rail 576, Item 471,* The National Archive, Kew
56 A simple and rugged key shaped device patented by J.E.Annett of the LBSCR
57 See also Appendix VIII
58 *Rail576, Item 428,* The National Archive, Kew
59 *Preston Chronicle,* 13 July 1872
60 *Rail 576, Items 1775, 1816, 1856,* The National Archive, Kew
61 *Preston Chronicle,* 11 July 1868
62 *Memorial to the Longridge Board of Health. LRO PR1637/1640*
63 *Rail 576, Item 1515,* The National Archive, Kew
64 *Rail 576, Item 1745,* The National Archive, Kew
65 *Preston Herald,* 6 June 1885
66 *Preston Herald,* 3 June 1885
67 *Preston Pilot,* 2 May 1840
68 *Preston Pilot,* 17 June 1848
69 *Preston Guardian,* 1849
70 *Preston Chronicle,* 5 July 1856
71 *Preston Chronicle,* March 1858
72 *Preston Chronicle,* 16 July 1859
73 *Preston Pilot,* 20 December 1865
74 *Preston Guardian,* 22 December 1866
75 *Preston Chronicle,* 31 August 1867
76 *Preston Chronicle,* 27 July 1867
77 *Preston Chronicle,* 10 October 1891
78 *Preston Chronicle,* 10 October 1892
79 *Preston Chronicle,* 10 September 1892
80 *Preston Chronicle,* 22 February 1865
81 'Life in Preston', *Preston Chronicle,* 11 February 1865
82 *Rail 576, Item 1674,* The National Archive, Kew
83 *Rail 576, Item 1882,* The National Archive, Kew
84 Letter kindly supplied by Syd Wood of Longridge
85 *Preston Guardian,* 22 May 1915
86 *Preston Guardian,* 8 June 1929
87 Smith, T. *History of Longridge,* (1888)

88   LRO DDX1162/3
89   Based on Bowtell, H. *Lesser Railways of Bowland Forest and Craven Country*, (Plateway Press, 1988)
90   *Rail 576*, The National Archive, Kew
91   Information concerning excursions is kindly supplied by Brian Bamber of Longridge
92   Information per David Eaves, March 2008
93   *Rail AN 155/14*, The National Archive, Kew
94   *Rail AN 155/14*, The National Archive, Kew
95   Courtesy: of Commercial Mapping Services, Network Rail, Manchester
96   *Lancashire Evening Post*
97   Courtesy: Martin Willacy (2005), who worked in the parcels office at Longridge Station
98   See also *Stevenson Locomotive Society Journal*, March 1980, p.78.
99   Jackson, B. *Steaming Ambitions*, (Triangle Publishing, 1999) pp.67-69. Reproduced by kind permission of Dennis Sweeney (Triangle Publishing)
100 *Preston Chronicle*, 12 June 1852
101 *A Pictorial Record of LNWR Signalling*, Richard D Foster
102 The LNWR used standard sizes for their signal boxes, size 'H' being 26ft 6in x 12ft.
103 The LNWR tumbler-frame was one of the most successful frame designs, the tumbler prevented the 'stirrup' catch handle from being moved if the lever was locked, thereby preventing the lever from being operated.
104 Sectional Appendix Western Division March 1937 LM&SR
105 'Single goods line' worked by one engine in steam, or two or more engines coupled together (Section VI of rule book).
106 Sectional Appendix Western Division March 1937 LM&SR
107 Sectional Appendix Western Division March 1937 LM&SR
108 London Midland Region Sectional Appendix Western Lines October 1960 British Railways
109 Sectional Appendix Western Division March 1937 LM&SR
110 Sectional Appendix Western Division March 1937 LM&SR
111 Sectional Appendix Western Division March 1937 LM&SR